SOCIAL WORK
IN PRIVATE PRACTICE
Principles, Issues, and Dilemmas

Robert L. Barker

NASW PRESS

National Association of Social Workers
Silver Spring, Maryland

Library of Congress Cataloging in Publication Data

Main entry under title:

Barker, Robert L.
   Social work in private practice.

   Bibliography: p.
   Includes index.
   1. Social workers—Practice—United States. 2. Social workers, Professional ethics for. I. National Association of Social Workers. II. Title.
HV10.5.B34 1984   361.3'068   84-8434
ISBN 0-87101-123-9

Printed in U.S.A.

Cover design by Cheryl Collins
Interior design by Dan Hildt

table
of contents

Robert L. Barker holds a DSW degree from the School of Social Work, Columbia University, New York City. He has been a private practitioner since 1969 and is on the faculty of the National Catholic School of Social Service, Catholic University of America, Washington, D.C. His next book, Treating Couples in Crisis, *is being published by Free Press (Macmillan Publishing Co.) in 1984.*

1
FOUNDATIONS OF PRIVATE PRACTICE

S he was just 29. Had little education. Only experience to speak of was office work. And the most serious problem of all—she was female. A woman in 1891 when women were not even considered as candidates to run large organizations. Especially not in a rough, bawdy port city such as Baltimore. But she was good with people. Had a knack for organizing them. Was very capable as a teacher and public speaker. Most important, she was honest. The men who had founded the local Charity Organization Society (COS) several years ago had no doubt about that. They had hired her as their bookkeeper and were very pleased with her work. They had promoted her to assistant treasurer just last year. Now they needed a new director, and they wondered if they should offer such a demanding job to this young lady. Mary Richmond was her name.

The men were ambivalent. The job would be challenging even for a man, even for someone with experience. Poverty was everywhere, and there was no public money to help. Only private philanthropy was keeping thousands from the almshouse. The Charity Organization Society had been established to solicit funds and distribute money and advice to the needy. Mary Richmond did a lot of this work herself when she could get away from her bookkeeping duties. Always eager to learn, she spent most of her free time studying and talking with people about how to be an effective helper. The men realized she had already proved herself. They decided to offer her the job.

As the chief executive officer of the Baltimore Charity Organization Society, young Mary Richmond found herself working harder than ever with the poor and the rich, with volunteers and employees, with drunken sailors and respectable merchants who were down on their luck because of the recent depression. The Baltimore COS, like the others around the nation, primarily utilized the services of volunteers. Most of these people were affluent, concerned socialites who had some spare time on their hands. They came to be known as "friendly visitors," and they talked with the needy and decided whom they would help.[1] But their work was unsystematic, and they were uncertain about how to do it well. Mary Richmond was often the only person in the office they could consult. They appreciated Mary Richmond's taking time to teach them. She taught them that people often needed more than money, that they also needed encouragement and advice on where to get jobs or relevant education, where to find affordable homes, how to get landlords to make repairs, how to unite the neighbors to help one another.

Before long, many of the contributors and volunteers recognized the worth of Mary Richmond's advice and its applicability to themselves as well as their clients. She was bright, understanding, a good listener. Many shared their problems with her: "Miss Richmond, please don't utter a word about this, but my daughter is in the family way." "Miss Richmond, could you come talk with my wife tonight? She is becoming insufferable and I shan't be able to tolerate it much longer." "Miss Richmond, I think my husband is possessed by Demon Rum and I wish you could help free him of this vile affliction."

One evening after the office was closed for the day, Mary Richmond was in her office catching up on her correspondence. There was a knock on the door, and it turned out to be one of the volunteers. The woman said she had personal problems and wanted Mary Richmond's help. After the talk, the grateful woman offered three dollars. Mary Richmond was perplexed. Should she take money for her services? Would it be proper? Ethical? She was on salary with COS. But the money was offered for her private work, not for the usual services of the organization. The woman who offered the money was not a COS client. Three dollars was half a week's pay! Mary Richmond could use the money. She could use it to help other clients. So, in 1895 Mary Richmond, one of the founders of professional social work, accepted the money for private practice.[2]

Years later, after she had trained countless social workers and had helped establish many of the principles and values that are now inherent in the profession,[3] she wrote this about private practice:

> How rapidly social casework will develop a private practice of its own cannot be predicted, but it should be evident from the examples given in this book that the skill here described can be utilized quite as well in the homes of the rich as in those of the poor, that in the one as in the other, personality can be thwarted and retarded, developed and enriched.[4]

Forty-Year Debate

When a leader of an organization or movement practices and condones an activity, the followers tend to embrace, sustain, nurture, and encourage its evolution from insignificance to maturity. After Mary Richmond was gone, however, much of social work seemed antipathetic toward private practice. It was treated almost as an illegitimate child, a bastard to ignore and disavow, lest acknowledgment disgrace its parents. For the next forty years, from the 1920s to the 1960s, the parents bickered and debated about what to do with this little creature, scarcely noticing that it was becoming larger and more independent on its own without much support or encouragement. By the 1960s it became too large to ignore, and its presence was no longer avoidable. Private practice could be treated as an orphan no longer.

During these forty years not everyone in social work wanted to disavow private practice, but the advocates were sparse and the opponents were persuasive. Besides, everyone agreed that there were far more important issues for social work. Public help for the disadvantaged was virtually nonexistent, and the needy had little choice but to turn to private agencies. Before 1930 there was an efflorescence of social agencies and a severe shortage of trained workers for the many new facilities. Membership in the nascent social work profession was increasing dramatically in all sections of the country.[5] Professional schools were being created; new ideas and techniques were being discovered and utilized. The profession had little time or room to develop private practice systematically. Little attention was given to those who might have wanted to provide their services outside the agencies.

Nevertheless, some would not be ignored. In 1926 a Philadelphia social worker decided to enter private practice. Seeking encouragement and ideas from her colleagues before taking the plunge, she went to her professional organization, the Philadelphia chapter of the American Association of Social Workers (AASW). The members listened to her idea, pondered its implications, and debated its merits. Finally, the group decided not to endorse her entry into private practice. There were no criteria, no norms, no qualifications to use as a basis for taking such a step. The members declared that there could be no such thing as private practice until standards and qualifications could be established by the profession.

The social worker was unhappy with the decision and persistent in keeping the issue alive at subsequent meetings. At her continued behest, the chapter contacted national AASW headquarters for an opinion. The AASW agreed with the chapter and would not sanction anyone as a private practitioner until more facts were obtained. A memo, which is still on file in the archives of the National Association of Social Workers (NASW), was sent to the Philadelphia chapter saying that the private practice of social work was a contradiction and that, without auspices, what was being practiced was something other than social work.[6] Private practice would have to wait.

But many social workers did not want to wait. NASW files contain numerous references to the activities of private social work practitioners in the 1930s.[7] Some workers requested guidance on how much to charge. Some asked what they should do to get more referrals, what their relationship with social agencies should be, how they could get professional sanction. Some writers wanted to know what they should call themselves. One letter, from a Seattle private practitioner, wondered if it was acceptable to be known as a "consultant on human relationships."

The first person known to publish anything about her personal experiences in private practice was Lee Steiner. In 1934 she "hung out her shingle."[8] Although she had received a master's degree in social work and wanted to indicate her degree along with a designation of social worker on her signs, she was not permitted to do so.

Her landlord forbade it. He pictured his building being filled with derelicts and impoverished beggars seeking her services. He believed the other tenants would not want to share the building with a "social worker." Thus, he agreed to lease space to her only if she deleted any reference to her profession.

Lee Steiner also had problems with her professional organization. The AASW had still not sanctioned private practice, and her local colleagues disapproved of her plan to charge fees for her services. Ironically, her landlord and fellow tenants held her in higher esteem and were less reluctant to lease space when they learned of her fee-charging plans. It must be remembered that fee charging by agencies and agency social workers was almost unknown at the time.[9] (The Jewish Family Services of New York City was one of the very first social agencies to charge fees, and it did not do so until 1943.)

Among other obstacles Lee Steiner faced was the problem of acquiring clients. Potential referral sources were not accustomed to recommending social workers. There was no listing for social workers in the telephone book, and the state had no certification or licensing for the profession. Advertising was then considered unethical. Most of Lee Steiner's referrals came from her professional colleagues in social agencies. Still, not as many came as she might have liked. Admitting that the experiment resulted in financial insecurity, she abandoned the project after two difficult years. "One person," she wrote, "cannot set precedents for an entire profession; she might attempt a few experiments but the profession itself would have to decide upon the validity of those experiments."[10] Lee Steiner returned to agency work for a brief time, but, having been bitten by the private practice bug, she left social work, returned to school, and became a certified psychologist. She eventually established her own successful private practice but in a different profession.

There were still only a handful of private practitioners before World War II, and they were often secretive about it.[11] Most did private practice part time while working days in agencies; they feared their full-time jobs would be in jeopardy if their moonlighting ventures were too conspicuous. They feared, too, the rejection of their social work colleagues. Many referred to themselves as psychotherapists, lay analysts, counselors—almost anything but "social worker."

Some gradually moved away from social work and into professions more hospitable to their private practices. Those who retained social work identities continued to ask their professional association for guidelines, sanctions, standards, and recognition.

Most of the professional leaders of the time disparaged the private practice movement and declared that it was inappropriate for the field of social work. This view remained strong through the 1950s.[12] Helen Perlman, for example, wrote, "As a private practitioner without an institutional connection, [a social worker] can make no formalized contribution to the development of social casework."[13] Another leader in the profession, Ruth Smalley, stated categorically, "Social work, as I understand it, is always practiced under some agency auspice."[14] Without the approbation of their profession, the small number of private practitioners faced many difficulties. They were not unified and thus had little influence to obtain sanctions within the profession. Perhaps it should not be surprising, then, that many others followed Lee Steiner's example and moved to other professions. Ironically, this became a major justification for many opponents of private practice to try to push the movement out of the profession on the basis that private practitioners had no social work identity or interest. Private practice was caught in a self-fulfilling prophecy.

There were a few exceptions. Some practitioners were finding success in private work, and in some cities they were unifying their forces. Ruth Fizdale organized a large and successful private practice group in New York in the early 1950s, and she documented the organization's experiences in several articles in the professional literature.[15] In other cities, some private practitioners began meeting regularly to discuss their common concerns. They were not yet recognized by their professional associations, but their influence in some local jurisdictions began to increase. The first public licensing of social work practice took place in San Diego, California, in 1952, largely through the efforts of one such group. Several other municipalities and states followed suit in the next few years, primarily because of the interest and influence of similar private practice groups.

Systematic analyses of private practice also started to occur in the 1950s.[16] The first studies confirmed the prevailing impression that private practitioners usually identified with professions other than social work, had more education and experience than their agency-based counterparts, and claimed they were practicing psychotherapy rather than social work.[17] They usually called their clients "patients," and most of their referrals came from psychiatrists. Even though such findings did not lead to much sympathy for private practice by agency-based social workers, the findings were crucial to the movement. They described what private practitioners were doing and what kind of workers were doing it. This was an essential step toward establishing norms and standards for private practice. These social workers helped make it possible for the profession to recognize private practice.

Advent of Professional Recognition

With increasing recognition, systematic analysis, and growing numbers of workers entering private practice, those who had long been frustrated in their efforts to obtain professional recognition became more hopeful in 1956. In that year, the seven major social work organizations merged to form NASW. Many practitioners hoped this new organization would include private practice under its auspices, but their hopes diminished quickly when the first NASW president, Nathan Cohen, made his inaugural statement to the membership. Commenting on the growing interest in private practice, he said he doubted whether private practitioners were any longer engaged in doing social work.[18]

Many members disagreed. Several local NASW chapters and individuals immediately began calling for the association to accept and develop standards for private social work practice. The association was still in its infancy, however, and more concerned with reorganizing its historical fields of practice. Besides, NASW replied, it could not determine if private work were a legitimate part of social work practice until social work practice itself was formally defined.[19] This "working definition of social work practice" was a priority of the young organization, and it was developed when NASW was a year old.[20] The definition enabled the profession to recognize private social work practice officially in 1958 and to acknowledge formally that private practice was an appropriate part of social work practice.[21]

In 1961 NASW formally endorsed the following definition of private practice:

> A private practitioner is a social worker who, wholly or in part, practices his profession outside the aegis of a governmental or duly incorporated voluntary agency, who has responsibility for his own practice and sets up his own conditions of exchange with his clients and identifies himself as a social work practitioner in offering his services.[22]

Shortly after the definition was released, NASW issued a policy statement to elaborate on private practice. It stated in part: "Practice within socially sponsored organizational structures must remain the primary avenue for the implementation of the goals of the profession.... NASW...avoids any action that will set apart or establish a special status, negative or positive, for private practice."[23]

Private practitioners might well have breathed a collective sigh of relief with these developments. At last they existed! They were finally acknowledged and sanctioned by their profession, albeit reservedly. There was some dissatisfaction with both the definition and the subsequent policy statement, but many practitioners took a "beggars can't be choosers" stance. Their dissatisfaction lay in the belief that the definition was inconsistent with the policy. For example, the policy stressed that private workers would have no status apart from the profession, yet the tone of the definition seemed to say that the private practitioner was an outsider. By definition, he or she was "outside a government or private agency." Many also questioned the necessity to identify themselves as social workers to be a part of the profession. Because many private practitioners had not previously referred to themselves as social workers, the issue was important and controversial. In any event, this definition and policy has remained essentially unchanged to date.

NASW's minimum standards for a social worker's entry into private practice were ratified in 1962. To become a professionally sanctioned private practitioner, one had to have a master's degree from an accredited school of social work, be professionally certified in the Academy of Certified Social Workers (ACSW), and have five years of acceptable, full-time, supervised agency employment. The supervision and experience had to be in the specialty of one's private practice. These standards have been modified slightly since their inception, but ACSW membership has been the basic professional standard since 1971.

Debate Intensifies

Professional sanction and standards raised the consciousness of those who were opposed to private practice, and in the early 1960s the debate became more intense than it had been before or has been since that time. Ruth Fizdale, by then the preeminent private practitioner-writer, declared to the National Conference on Social Welfare in 1961 that there was increasing demand for private practitioners in social work.[24] She said this required the profession to develop systematic and enforced standards. Max Siporin, in an influential study about the roles of private practice, determined that social work could be practiced equally well in an agency or a private setting.[25]

The arguments against private practice tended to emphasize five points, which were summarized by Sherman Merle in his classic 1962 article, "Some Arguments Against Private Practice."[26] He suggested that private practice may be anathema to social work values because it discriminates against the less affluent; it does not provide services to those who are in need but unable to pay; it is so ill-defined that it needs agency auspices to provide norms and standards for the workers; it encourages workers to leave agencies, resulting in a shortage of manpower where the services are most needed. He contended even the title "private" practice of "social" work is contradictory, using words and concepts that are mutually exclusive. These arguments have been repeated in numerous statements for the twenty years since the Merle article appeared.[27] Ironically, Merle demonstrated his flexibility when he later became listed in the NASW *Register of Clinical Social Workers* as a "private practitioner."[28]

Of course, those in support of the private practice movement disputed these arguments. They pointed out that private practitioners need not be in agencies to be defined. They stressed the importance for anyone offering a service for a fee to be very specific about what is being offered and what the credentials are. Private practitioners, possibly even more than agency social workers, find it imperative to define their roles to each potential consumer of their services, or the consumer will not buy those services.

They also defended themselves against the charge that private practice was discriminatory. If discrimination meant that only certain segments of the population would be eligible for service, they pointed out, then agency workers also discriminate. Most agencies charge their clients fees, and the amount can be as high as any charged by private practitioners. When fees are flexible enough for all clients to pay, the social agency must then subject the applicant to a means test to determine the client's resources. Most social workers feel the means test is a highly questionable, discriminatory, or undesirable practice.[29] There are many established social agencies that serve ethnic or religious groups or select segments of the population such as the aged, the handicapped, the young, or those who live within certain geographic boundaries. These social agencies are also discriminatory, the defenders of private practice pointed out, but their criteria of discrimination has, with tradition, become acceptable.

Still, most private practitioners acknowledge the fundamental validity of the charge that some clients are excluded because of financial limitations. Many people on the lower side of the economic spectrum simply do not have access to the services of a private practitioner. This is true despite the practitioner's assertions and rationalizations that agencies also charge high fees, that insurance companies cover much of the costs of service, or that fees tend to be based on a sliding scale. The majority of private practitioners are not readily accessible geographically, socially, or financially to a significant portion of the economically disadvantaged.

Private practitioners also found it hard to refute the contention that the terms "private" and "social" are contradictory. Undoubtedly, the words do not sound right together. "Social" is an antonym for "private." Many practitioners, for that reason, want to call themselves "autonomous" or "independent" social work practitioners instead. These terms, however, have not caught on among social workers, probably because the other helping professions have used the private practice designation.

The last argument—that the private practice movement would draw needed social workers away from already understaffed agencies —has not occurred.[30] Such a concern was appropriate during the social work manpower shortages of prior decades, but, now that there is an ample supply of social work manpower brought about by many public funding cutbacks in those services provided by social workers, the fear is unfounded. There are few agencies that are unable to find well-educated, highly competent social work employees from among their many applicants.[31]

Professional Ambivalence

As the private practice movement has grown since the 1960s, the debate has diminished but not ended, nor does it seem likely to end in the foreseeable future. Social work's history and heritage, its values and aspirations for society, and its methods for reaching these goals place the private practice model of delivering social service at the center of a complex and possibly irreconcilable conflict. Social work is and has always been ambivalent about two systems inherent in private social work practice: the entrepreneurial or business approach to helping and the clinical or residual model of delivering services.

Private practice is a business, and social work has mixed feelings about business, its practices, goals, and consequences. Many social workers see the proponents of business as the enemy, the perpetrator of social disadvantage. If the systems were more equitable, social workers frequently say, if people had greater protection from capitalistic exploitation or business upheavals, then there would be far less suffering. The language of business, terms such as "free enterprise," "rugged individualism," "competition in the marketplace," and "profit motive," are seen by many social workers as shibboleths. Using such code words implies to many social workers that the user subscribes to the philosophy known as "social Darwinism," or survival of the economic fittest.[32] Many social workers are convinced that those who use such terms or endorse such concepts have a proclivity for exploiting the disadvantaged or, at least, are indifferent to the needy.

It is understandable why many in the profession hold this view.

The ubiquitous poverty and suffering that existed during the crea-
tion of social work was usually attributed to economic turmoil or
to conscious capitalistic exploitation. Since the beginning of their
profession, social workers have tried to combat the problems faced
by the economically disadvantaged. With such a heritage, it is little wonder that many social workers look at business practice as
the enemy. When they see many of their members entering private
practice, they are distressed. It seems tantamount to desertion. To
leave traditional social work for private practice, says this view, is
to weaken the cause and nourish the enemy.

The other source of social work ambivalence about private practice grows from the perennial conflict about the profession's social
function. Social workers have long debated whether to serve society by helping individuals cope more effectively with the unavoidable
problems of society or by seeking to bring about institutional
changes in society so individuals will not have to face those problems. The debate has had many different names through the
decades— "cause versus function," "social activism versus casework,"
"developmental versus residual intervention," "primary versus ter-
tiary prevention," "macro versus micro perspectives" —but the substantive issue remains the same. Most social workers, regardless of
what they do in practice, believe that achieving institutional change
is the fairest, most efficient, and most logical way to achieve professional objectives. Yet private social work practice is, or seems to be,
primarily a residual approach to problem solving. In other words,
the private practitioner enables the client to cope with or adjust to
a condition in society that caused the problem. The client seeks the
services of the worker after his problem has emerged. The social
institutions caused, or did not help overcome, the problem, so the
social worker helps the individual find better ways of coping with
this circumstance.

Of course, there is considerable merit in this view. At best, private practice can be only one of many ways to ameliorate problems.
It is not and does not pretend to be a cure-all. It will never have
more than a minor impact on the entire social welfare process. Major
emphasis may properly be placed on bringing about institutional
rather than residual improvements in the social welfare system, but
it is grandiose and naive to expect that there will not always be a

need for both. No utopian society can be created in which none of its members will have problems. As long as resources are finite, as long as no two people can agree on what is a perfect, problem-free society, there will be a need for the provision of residual services. Private practice will never be a particularly lofty ambition or that important in the social and historical scheme of things. At best, it will provide an important but ancillary service for some individuals.

It is not valid, however, to imply that because private practice has its limitations it should not be a part of social work. Neither agency-based practice or the "macro" approach of social work advocacy and policy development is without limitations. These models also have their critics.

The proponents of private practice ask what is wrong with peaceful coexistence and mutual support. The delivery of social services is a vastly complicated, ever-changing process, which requires a wide variety of people who employ a variety of techniques in heterogenous settings. A variegated approach leads to innovation, creativity, and greater efficacy, all sorely needed commodities, especially in the much beleagured profession of social work. Employing the best elements of agency-based and private practice is in the best interests of the client, the profession, and society.

Private Practice Today

Those who are unenthusiastic about private practice may not be swayed by the arguments above, but today they are confronted by another compelling factor. Whatever merits or demerits independent social work may have, it has become too large to be ignored and too influential to be wished away.[33] It took four decades for the movement to grow from a handful to a few hundred, but today thousands of social workers are hanging out their private practice shingles. Levenstein estimated that the number of social workers entering private practice has doubled every five years since 1925.[34]

How many private practitioners are there? This has always been conjectural. Obtaining accurate statistics is impeded by two factors. One is that the definition of private practice does not precisely distinguish between who is and who is not a private practitioner. Therefore, the number of social workers said to be in private practice has varied depending on which of the many possible definitions and criteria are used. (The issues of definition and criteria are of such importance that they will be addressed in the next chapter.)

The other factor is that private practitioners have tended to be independent and, therefore, they are not easy to count. Many are not affiliated with any social work organizations or groups that would include them in statistical records. Many do not list themselves as social workers but identify themselves with other psychotherapy-providing professions. Many others belong to social work organizations other than NASW, organizations whose focus is on clinical work and private practice. The most influential of these organizations have been I-CAPP (International Conference for the Advancement of Private Practice) and the National Federation of Societies for Clinical Social Work, publisher of the journal *Clinical Social Work.* Many have joined these groups because of the perceived antipathy toward private and clinical social work practice by the social work "establishment." Other social workers in private practice join non-social work organizations such as the American Association for Marriage and Family Therapy, the International Group Psychotherapy Association, and the American Psychotherapy Association. These and many other groups are open to several professional groups in mental health services and, in some cases, their membership rolls have a high percentage of social workers. Others belong to more than one of these organizations and are possibly being counted more than once.

It is even difficult to determine the number of private practitioners among the members of NASW. The 1982 NASW *Register of Clinical Social Workers* listed over 4,500 social workers as having private practice as their primary employment; however, many private practitioners are excluded if they choose not to pay the fee for listing.[35] The register also includes practitioners who are not members of NASW. Some who are listed as private practitioners may be seeing few or no clients; still others are in private practice but use a corporate name for identification. It is difficult to distinguish in the register between those who are salaried agency-based workers and those who receive fees for services using corporate office names.

Therefore, whenever estimates about the numbers of private practitioners are given, they must be scrutinized carefully. The numbers have varied widely and sometimes can reflect the bias of the estimator. Proponents of private practice have tended to assume the numbers are high, and opponents have suggested the numbers are miniscule. In 1954, for example, Ruth Smalley estimated that there were fewer than 100 private social work practitioners.[36] In 1962, when the profession sanctioned private practice, it was estimated that between 1,700 and 2,000 practitioners were at work full- or part-time across the nation.[37] In 1967, the NASW Committee on Private Practice calculated that 3,000 to 4,000 practitioners were so engaged.[38] Nine years later, the NASW executive director testified that there were between 8,500 and 10,000 social workers in private practice.[39] In 1982, the NASW *Register of Clinical Social Workers* included 8,991 names, of whom at least 4,500 (as noted previously) listed private practice as their primary employment. Such figures are important clues about the growth of private practice but cannot be taken as conclusive statements about the number of practitioners.

At any rate, social workers in private practice are clearly growing in numbers and influence, whatever the specific count. Any further argument about whether private practice should or does exist is irrelevant.

Notes and References

1. Mary Richmond, *Friendly Visiting among the Poor* (New York: Macmillan Co., 1899).

2. "Charities Record, 1896," as cited in Sidney Levenstein, *Private Practice in Social Casework: A Profession's Changing Pattern* (New York: Columbia University Press, 1964), p. 26.

3. Mary Richmond, *Social Diagnosis* (New York: Russell Sage Foundation, 1917), p. 27.

4. Mary Richmond, *What Is Social Casework?* (New York: Russell Sage Foundation, 1922), p. 221.

5. Roy Lubove, *The Professional Altruist: The Emergence of Social Work as a Career 1890–1930* (Cambridge, Mass: Harvard University Press, 1965), pp. 40–71.

6. American Association of Social Workers, Memorandum, May 3, 1926, as cited in Levenstein, *Private Practice in Social Casework,* p. 44.

7. Levenstein, *Private Practice in Social Casework,* p. 44.

8. Lee R. Steiner, "Hanging Out A Shingle," *Newsletter of the American Association of Psychiatric Social Workers,* 6 (Winter 1936), pp. 1–8. (Now *Journal of Psychiatric Social Work.)*

9. Nathaniel Goodman, "Fee Charging," *Encyclopedia of Social Work,* Vol. 1 (16th issue; New York: National Association of Social Workers, 1971), pp. 413–415.

10. Lee R. Steiner, "Casework as a Private Venture," *The Family,* 19 (March 1938), pp. 188–196.

11. Myron Rockmore, "Private Practice: An Exploratory Inquiry," *Survey,* 84 (1948), pp. 109–111.

12. Margaret A. Golton, "Private Practice in Social Work," *Encyclopedia of Social Work,* Vol. 2 (16th issue; New York: National Association of Social Workers, 1971), pp. 949–955.

13. Helen Perlman et al., "Psychotherapy and Counseling," *Annals of the New York Academy of Sciences,* 63 (1955), pp. 319–432.

14. Ruth Smalley, "Can We Reconcile Generic Education and Specialized Practice?" *Journal of Psychiatric Social Work,* 23 (January 1954), pp. 207–217.

15. Ruth Fizdale, "Formalizing the Relationship between Private Practitioners and Social Agencies," *Social Casework,* 40 (November 1959).

16. Rowena Ryerson and Elizabeth Weller, "The Private Practice of Psychiatric Social Work," *Journal of Psychiatric Social Work,* 16, No. 2 (1947), pp. 110–116.

17. Josephine Peek and Charlotte Plotkin, "Social Caseworkers in Private Practice," *Smith College Studies in Social Work,* 21 (March 1951), pp. 165–197.

18. Nathan E. Cohen, "A Changing Profession in a Changing World," *Social Work,* 1 (October 1956), p. 16.

19. Thomas L. Briggs, "Private Practice," Memorandum to Chapter Chairmen, Document No. 3832/1/5 (New York: National Association of Social Workers, 1961), pp. 1–4. (Mimeographed.)

20. Harriett M. Bartlett, "Toward Clarification and Improvement of Social Work Practice," *Social Work,* 3 (April 1958), pp. 3–9.

21. *Handbook on the Private Practice of Social Work* (Washington, D.C.: National Association of Social Workers, 1974), pp. 39–40.

22. Ibid., p. 40.

23. Ibid., p. 45.

24. Ruth Fizdale, "The Rising Demand for Private Casework Services," *Social Welfare Forum, 1961* (New York: National Conference on Social Welfare and Columbia University Press, 1961), pp. 194–204.

25. Max Siporin, "Private Practice of Social Work: Functional Roles and Social Control," *Social Work,* 6 (April 1961), pp. 52–60.

26. Sherman Merle, "Some Arguments Against Private Practice," *Social Work,* 7 (January 1962), pp. 12–17.

27. See, for example, Elizabeth Howe, "Public Professions and the Private Model of Professionalism," *Social Work,* 25 (May 1980), pp. 179–191.

28. *NASW Register of Clinical Social Workers* (3d ed.; Silver Spring, Md.: National Association of Social Workers, 1982), p. 628.

29. Walter C. Bentrup, "The Profession and the Means Test," *Social Work,* 9 (April 1964), pp. 10–17.

30. Francis Turner, *Psychosocial Therapy: A Social Work Perspective* (New York: Free Press, 1978), p. 179.

31. Robert L. Barker, "Supply Side Economics in Private Psychotherapy Practice: Some Ominous and Encouraging Trends," *Psychotherapy in Private Practice,* 1 (Spring 1983), pp. 71–81.

32. Richard Hofstader, *Social Darwinism in American Thought* (Philadelphia: University of Pennsylvania Press, 1944).

33. Marquis Earl Wallace, "Private Practice: A Nationwide Study," *Social Work,* 27 (May 1982), pp. 262–267.

34. Levenstein, *Private Practice in Social Casework,* p. 151.

35. *NASW Register of Clinical Social Workers.*

36. Smalley, "Can We Reconcile Generic Education and Specialized Practice?" p. 208.

37. Levenstein, *Private Practice in Social Casework.*

38. Golton, "Private Practice in Social Work," p. 952.

39. Chauncey Alexander, "Testimony to Subcommittee on Comprehensive Coverage" (New York: Health Insurance Association of America, 1976), pp. 1–4. (Mimeographed.)

2

ELEMENTS OF
PRIVATE PRACTICE

What is private practice in social work? To be considered a private practitioner, must one be a clinician? Must one be a member of NASW and ACSW? Can someone be a private practitioner without a license, clients, or an advanced professional degree? The term has been so value laden, controversial, and ill-defined in the past that it seems to have taken on a variety of different meanings. For example, social workers themselves are not always enlightening when they are asked if they are private practitioners: One might say yes and another no, even though both are doing identical work in identical settings.

Some social workers identify themselves as private practitioners even though they are salaried by agencies, because their agencies are funded through private contributions.[1] Some see themselves as private practitioners even though they are salaried social workers employed by other private practitioners. Some identify themselves as such, whether or not they have any clients or are qualified, simply because they are unemployed. Some social workers who are employed by social agencies consider themselves private practitioners because the agency pays them on a fee-for-service basis like independent contractors. Some do not consider themselves to be in private practice, even though they receive fees for service, because they do not work out of an office or clinical setting. They may be industrial consultants or community organizers and are completely self-employed. Others say they are not private practitioners because they work primarily in social work agencies and see only a few clients on their own time just to keep in touch.

The variations in practice models seem endless, and the difficulty in specifying what is and is not private practice is challenging. It is reminiscent of the decision confronting the U.S. Supreme Court about pornography, leading Justice Potter Stewart to say, "I may not be able to define it, but I sure know it when I see it."

Social workers believe they know what private practice is when they see it, but there is not consensus about how it is to be defined. It is little wonder, therefore, that there is so much difficulty in determining how many social workers are in private practice. Thus, it would seem useful to specify the subject matter of this book, and the following definition of private practice is offered:

> Private social work practice is the process in which the values, knowledge, and skills of social work, which were acquired through sufficient education and experience, are used to deliver social services autonomously to clients in exchange for mutually agreed payment.

Criteria for Private Practice

Any definition is merely a skeleton. Considerable filling out must take place before one really grasps what private social work practice is. Criteria must be established to state who is and is not in private practice. The criteria used in this book includes ten norms: The private practitioner

1. has the client as the primary obligation;
2. determines who the client will be;
3. determines the techniques to be used in service to this client;
4. determines practice professionally, not bureaucratically;
5. receives a fee for service directly from or in behalf of the client;
6. is educated as a social worker;
7. is a sufficiently experienced social worker;
8. adheres to social work values, standards, and ethics;
9. is licensed, certified, and registered, where applicable, to engage in private practice; and
10. is professionally responsible.

Each of these norms will be discussed in order to fill out the definition. Comparisons are made between the agency worker and the private practitioner in the case of each norm. Making the comparison does not imply that one or the other model of delivering social services is necessarily the best; both have their virtues and limitations with respect to these characteristics.

Primary Obligation

The NASW Code of Ethics states, in Section II-F, that "The social worker's primary responsibility is to clients." [2] That principle is more difficult to follow than it seems. Employees of any organization are obliged to fulfill the conditions of employment; it is unreasonable to expect most employees, whatever the standards of their profession, to place something else above this obligation. As Piliavin has pointed out, the agency employee will generally conform to the policies and work requirements of the agency rather than the needs of a given client if there is conflict over whose interests have precedence.[3]

Many agency-based workers would dispute this contention if it is made in the abstract. The issue is rarely tested, fortunately, because agency requirements and those of clients are, in fact, generally compatible. However, when specific and live, rather than hypothetical, events are considered, the principle looks more questionable. An agency policy, for example, might be to maintain a waiting list for potential clientele; but suppose that an individual could not wait his or her turn. If the worker knows service is needed but also knows that agency policy is firm, what can be done? Consider another example: A client may begin receiving service from an agency that has a policy of providing services only for short amounts of time in order to be available to as many people as possible. When the time limit is reached, if the client still requires the service, what is the worker likely to do? Certainly, in these examples, there would be some flexibility in agency policy, but if the flexibility becomes so loose as to result in a cessation of that policy, the agency could begin a tightening-up process. If the worker took advantage of the flexibility and continued to make exceptions, he or she is not likely to remain in the employer's favor. Eventually, there would be enough pressure on the worker to assure subsequent conformity to agency policy above all other considerations or the worker would not remain at the agency. As Noll writes: "Whenever the mental health professional is employed by an agency or by an institution, the institution's needs will almost invariably

supersede those of the patient. There is a basic, usually unacknowl-
edged, antagonistic relationship between the individual and the institutional professional."[4]

The private practice model of delivering social services has less
problem than agency-based practice with this dilemma. The principle of client precedence is unquestionable for the private social
worker except in very rare and highly unusual circumstances. The
first and foremost distinguishing characteristic of private practice
is that the practitioner is an employee of the client. The practitioner
may be fired or replaced at any time for any reason if the work is
not satisfactory to the client. The agency-based worker can be fired
only if the work is unsatisfactory to the agency. The client has the
same authority over the private practitioner as would any other
employer, so the worker is faced with fewer conflicts about divided
loyalties. The client–private practitioner relationship is implemented,
or the worker is hired, when both reach an agreement that is
mutually satisfactory. This agreement, or contract, may be implicit
or explicit, but both parties come to it without manifest responsibility
to other auspices. It must be noted, however, that there may be some
risks in the private model that are often less serious in agencies.
The major threat to the client's interest would be the private practitioner's personal motivation to exploit or otherwise let personal interests predominate over the client's. The agency structure has more
checks and balances than private work and these help to decrease
the likelihood of such occurrences.

Selecting a Clientele

In the agency-based model of social work practice, the worker
typically is assigned clients, and the typical clients have less choice
about the worker they will see. The agency might have an intake
worker who determines which staff member would be most appropriate to see the client, or the decision might be made at random,
depending on which worker is next on the list. In smaller agencies,
where there may be only one or two workers, it is still agency policy
that determines which worker sees a given client. "One of the factors influencing the relative lack of choice," writes Francis Turner,
"has been our tradition of offering services as agents of society's
objectives and values, usually in a format where fees are not

involved. Serving social objectives first makes client self-determination of only secondary importance."[5]

Many agencies, but certainly not most, have recognized the importance of effective matching and have learned that worker-client interactions are significantly improved when care is taken. Matching refers to the exclusive or preferential assignment of certain types of clients to specific types of agency personnel.[6] Given the fact that some social workers deal more effectively with some clients than with others, it follows that some clients relate more effectively with some workers than with others. The matching process in many agencies, if any exists at all, often leaves much to be desired. In private practice, the matching process is carried out by the social worker and the client; the practitioner decides what type of client he or she works best with and targets practice to this type of clientele. The practitioner may pursue more knowledge about a given type of client or a given type of technique but makes the decision freely.

The risks inherent in this approach are readily apparent, however. Workers are not always able to judge their own competence. Most private practitioners cannot be objective about the clientele to exclude. Moreover, in the competitive marketplace situation inherent in private practice, some practitioners are inclined to see any client who seeks their services, regardless of whether or not they are capable of providing the needed service. This would be less likely to occur in the social agency, where the worker most capable of providing the service could be given the assignment.

Determining the Method of Service Delivery

Agency policy often predetermines the methods that are to be employed in providing service, and supervisors, because of the agency requirements, often require that the worker use a predetermined technique or provide a specific type of service. For example, some agencies are oriented to long-term, analytically based, insight-oriented treatments, while others provide short-term crisis intervention. Some specialize in helping people get jobs or financial supports; some use group therapy techniques, Transactional Analysis methods, or behavioral training programs. The agency worker is thus restricted in the type of method that can be used in the client's behalf.

In private practice, there are fewer restrictions about method. As a professional person who has the education, experience, skill, and knowledge to make decisions about the best approach and available treatment for any given problem, the private practitioner decides the method to use. The method is then explicated by the worker for the client's consent. Neither makes this decision with reference to agency requirements. If, for example, the worker ascertained that the client's problem would best be treated by involving the entire family in a Bowen Family Therapy model, it would be within the worker's province to recommend and possibly provide such treatment.[7] If, however, the worker is employed by an agency that subscribes to the structural/strategic family therapy approach, the worker would have difficulty using the Bowen method.

There are risks involved, however. The worker might be more inclined to prescribe treatments that are familiar, even though they may not be the best methods available. In an agency setting, this is less likely to happen. The major outside control on the private practitioner would be the possibility of malpractice litigation and legal and professional sanctions if the client is harmed.

Practicing Professionally, Not Bureaucratically

Organizations and social agencies use bureaucratic principles as their mode of operation. Divisions of labor, specialization, delegation of responsibility, and definition of roles to prevent overlap are among the essential components of bureaucracy and of any social work organization. Unlike private practitioners, "social workers [in agencies] are *bureaucrats*. In this role, the social worker is required to negotiate the stresses, opportunities, and constraints that permeate organizational life, regardless of what his position is in the organization."[8]

It is the nature of any organization to state what the expected behavior of its members is to be and to enforce conformity; this helps the organization to coordinate its activities and avoid disorganization. Thus, the agency worker's ability to make professional decisions is circumscribed within predetermined limits. In sum, practice is essentially bureaucratically, rather than professionally, determined. Professionalism and bureaucracy are not mutually exclusive, however, and there is ample opportunity for professional behavior to operate effectively within organizational limits.

Private practice is essentially nonorganizational. The independent practitioner does not spend a large portion of time engaged in organizational prerogatives, and behavior is limited only by professional requirements and personal judgments. Decisions affecting practice are circumscribed by the practitioner's professional organization and public statute. However, a private practitioner who chooses to ignore professional mores (which is, unfortunately, more easily done in private practice because of the lack of bureaucratic controls) can provide a disservice to those in need of help.

Fee-for-Service Income

The client pays the private practitioner to perform a specific service. The payment is related to that particular service; payment is not made for activities that do not directly benefit the client. For example, when the worker takes a special course to improve skills that can help the client, the client does not pay the worker directly for that training. The worker's income is dependent on the service provided, for which there is an agreement about payment. This contrasts with the agency-based model, in which payment is not based on service delivered but rather on conformity to the agency's expectations. The agency might require the worker to maintain regular hours, provide service for all assigned clients, attend workshops, and engage in administrative duties as part of the conditions of employment. In exchange for this conformity, the agency pays the worker a salary, money to which the worker is entitled regardless of how often any one client is seen.

One exception is the case in which an agency pays its employees on a per capita contractual basis. The amount paid is based on the number of clients seen. The worker receives fees for service, but the amount of the fee or the conditions of payment are set by the agency rather than the worker. The contractual worker is not engaged in private practice, despite fees for service, because the worker does not fulfill the first three criteria.

Many social workers consider themselves private practitioners when they work on a contractual basis for a private practitioner. Actually, they are employees of the private practitioner, a relationship similar to a nurse who works for a private practice physician or a legal research assistant employed by a private attorney. Usually the employer is a well-established private practitioner who has more clients and referrals than he or she can see alone. This person may be a social worker or a member of another profession who recognizes the value of social service delivery to clients. This practitioner usually provides the office space and clients for the social worker and maintains overall responsibility for the case by reviewing and supervising the social worker's direct treatment of clients. The social worker is paid only a percentage of the amount paid by or in behalf of the client; the rest goes to the employing private practitioner. Less commonly, the social worker is paid a predetermined annual or monthly salary for providing services prescribed by the practitioner. This practice is becoming popular as a way to increase the practice and income of an established private practitioner, and it provides some social workers with jobs. To some, however, the activity borders on the questionable practice of "fee splitting." Government peer review organizations and third-party payers have been challenging the practice with increasing regularity and success. The social worker as well as the client is possibly being exploited. In any event, the contractual worker in this circumstance is not a private practitioner.

Education

Private practice is very demanding. It requires the worker to make frequent, rapid, and independent judgments without much help from others. There are no supervisors to add ideas to the decision-making process in private practice. No agency or clinic policies exist to predetermine what kind of clients to serve or what methods to use. The private practitioner is more visible as an individual to the public than is the worker employed in an agency. Thus, knowledge at ready command to make these judgments is crucial, and the social worker's professional education provides both the theoretical and practical foundation for being able to make such independent judgments.[9] Social work education is practical as well as conceptual, qualities most important for private work.[10] Engaging in private practice with only a theoretical foundation could be hazardous to the client as well as to the worker. It would be like playing on a professional basketball team after having read books on how the game should be played but never having played it. It also takes practice, trial and error, and a considerable amount of coaching to be able to carry out the right plays.

The amount and kind of social work education necessary to engage in private practice is debatable. Most states that license social workers for independent practice specify that the practitioners must possess at least a master's degree in social work from an accredited graduate school. NASW and other professional social work organizations that sanction private practice also require the MSW as the minimum educational standard. Whether a two-year graduate program is enough formal education for private social work practice is being debated by social work groups as well as government funding organizations and third-party financers; this question is being raised largely because of other professions that provide mental health services. They point out that the doctorate is their minimum requirement, that it takes this level of education to provide adequate services, and that the minimum requirement of a master's degree in social work is competitively unfair to them. Some schools of social work are already looking at the possibility of a doctorate for practice, and it is quite possible that this degree will eventually become the minimum educational requirement for social work too.[11]

Practice Experience

Regardless of the quality and extent of one's education, the social worker requires substantial practical experience to consolidate and integrate that training. The profession of social work has long recognized that the master's degree is only a beginning step toward providing professional social services, that supervised practice in an agency is essential. This provides a safeguard for clients and makes it possible to assure them that they are, directly or indirectly, in the hands of competent professionals.[12] Professional ethics and personal consideration for the client's well-being should dictate that the social worker acquire substantial agency-based supervision in the beginning practice years. Until the practitioner has the background to make independent decisions and implement techniques autonomously, he or she is dependent on the supervisor's experience and wisdom.

Many practitioners believe that the supervision requirement has been overdone in agency settings. In private practice, however, it is rarely overdone but is in considerable danger of being underdone.

There seems to be a trend toward relaxing this requirement in agency work. One recent study revealed that 75 percent of the social workers sampled who had graduated from schools of social work since 1967 had received little or no supervision.[13] The danger of this trend occurs when the relatively inexperienced social worker enters private practice with no further supervision. Without objective professional observation, the practitioner is more vulnerable to developing bad professional habits and blind spots. It must be remembered that the practitioner represents the profession to the public, and mistakes could be viewed by consumers of services as representative of the profession. This is not to suggest that a recent social work graduate could not work under supervision in a private practitioner's office; in this instance, the graduate would not be working autonomously but would be gathering the necessary experience, just as in a social work agency, to work independently eventually.

How much time is enough? How long must a social worker be supervised before being considered capable of autonomous practice? There is no single answer to these questions. The NASW professional standard is based on the ACSW requirement of two years of paid social work employment or 3,000 hours of paid, part-time experience. The ACSW requirement says that it is desirable, although not required, that this work is done under the direct supervision of an ACSW social worker.[14] Another ACSW requirement includes professional references, with one from the worker's present immediate supervisor. Most of the states that now license social workers have followed the NASW recommendation on the amount of required experience. Nevertheless, some state licensing requirements include no provisions for experience, although several others require more than two years of experience before sanctioning private practice. Obviously, the social worker will need to conform to the state legal regulations before considering entry into private practice.

Social Work Values and Ethics

The NASW Code of Ethics is "based on the fundamental values of the social work profession that include the worth, dignity, and uniqueness of all persons as well as their rights and opportunities. It is also based on the nature of social work, which fosters conditions that promote these values."[15] Thus, ethics and values are so integral to the nature of the profession that the profession is meaningless without them. The image that the social worker presents to the public is that the profession's values and ethics are designed to enhance the client's well-being. The worker who deviates from those values and ethical standards may be engaged in private practice but not necessarily in social work private practice. The Code of Ethics represents to the public and to consumers of private social work services a standard of behavior to which the practitioner is obligated; without such a commitment, the practitioner cannot lay claim to membership within the field.

Licensing and Certification

A license is a credential awarded to an individual who meets certain qualifications established by the public in the form of a legal statute. The purpose of a license, in theory at least, is to protect the public. It is assumed that the applicant for the license engages in complex activities that are difficult for a potential consumer to evaluate independently. The state thus provides an a priori evaluation for the consumer. The state says that the license holder has met its standards and accordingly is qualified to provide the service. It is, therefore, in the interests of the profession, its clients, and its members to have licensing wherever social work practice exists. NASW has made it official policy to pursue licensing of social work practice in each state and, in recent years, has intensified its efforts toward achieving that goal.[16]

Certification is the credential awarded to a qualified individual by a professional organization for meeting its standards. The purpose, although not usually stated as such, is to protect the profession as well as the client. It is to protect the title "certified social worker" and to demonstrate to the public that anyone with that designation has fulfilled certain requirements. Social workers, whether or not they are in states that have licensing, must become professionally certified if they are to be sanctioned for private practice by NASW. In nonlicensed states and the District of Columbia, a private practitioner may legally work without a license, but he or she would have considerable difficulty getting much professional support and acceptance by third-party financing organizations without at least the professional certificate.

There are considerable problems with social work licenses and certificates. Hardcastle has evaluated the existing licensing regulations; he found that in every state they are so unspecific and imprecise that they have little potential for protection of the public or the profession and need substantial strengthening.[17] This is a product not of legislative indecisiveness but of the difficulty in defining with precision what it is that social workers do and what skills are required to do it.[18] Social workers might wonder, then, what difference it makes whether or not they have a license or certificate. As a practical matter, it would be illegal to practice social work in some places without one or the other.

Professional Responsibility and Accountability

Professional responsibility and the maintenance of standards that are in keeping with the highest tradition of social work are implicit in all the above criteria, but their importance is such that it also needs to be made explicit. The private practitioner, in making independent judgments and in implementing decisions about practice, is primarily responsible for those actions and accountable for their success. The private practitioner does not have the protective blanket that often exists for the agency-based worker, who shares responsibility with colleagues, supervisors, agency administrators, and agency policy. Accordingly, the private worker must answer to the public and the profession for any actions that are below standard or not in keeping with the best interest of the client. The private practitioner is putting his or her abilities, knowledge, and behavior on the line with every contact made with a client. This requires diligence and a high commitment to responsible action according to the standards of social work practice.[19] The agency-based worker is typically expected to behave according to those same standards, but the enforcement of those behaviors comes from agency policy, supervisors, and administrators rather than from only the practitioner.

Social workers, whether they are employed in agencies or in private practice, whether their primary orientation is clinical treatment or prevention and institutional development, share a common purpose. It is "to promote or restore a mutually beneficial interaction between individuals and society in order to improve the quality of life for everyone."[20] Private practitioners, as a part of the profession, are not excused from this obligation, even though their occasional isolation from their colleagues might mean they have fewer reminders of the fact. Private social workers have at least as much opportunity, and probably more than most other social workers, to uphold this purpose. Freed from the constraints of cautious employers or restraints against political activism as faced by some government employees, they are in a good position to work toward these objectives. It is neither necessary for a private practitioner to be a clinician nor, if the practitioner is a clinician, to limit activity to clinical work. As a citizen and as a social worker, the practitioner has the opportunity to get outside the office and work to achieve the values to which the profession subscribes.

Private Practice as a Business

The ten norms of private social work practice noted earlier refer to professional issues. Another element, which is almost as important, is the nature of private practice as a business enterprise. To succeed in such a venture, the social worker must be more than a competent professional; he or she must also be a competent business person, knowing the principles of sound business, implementing them appropriately, and reconciling them with the values of the profession.

As a business enterprise, the private practice model of delivering social services has always had more in common with social agency service delivery than generally imagined.[21] There are and will always be significant differences, but of late the differences have been significantly reduced. The services of private practitioners have become available to a much wider portion of the economic spectrum than is generally realized, while agency services are becoming less accessible to many of those in need.

Because of severe financial pressures, many social work agencies have found themselves "disengaging from the poor."[22] They are charging their clients much higher fees and serving more affluent and well-insured clients; it has become more difficult for those with fewer resources to get their help. The fees charged the more affluent are often as high as those charged by private practitioners. Agencies are not doing this because they lack compassion for the needy, but because many of them could not survive otherwise. The costs of running an agency have become so great and governmental and philanthropic contributions have been so reduced that there is no alternative but to get funds from those served. Agency spokespeople point out, with ample justification, that they would be unable to serve even the smaller number of needy clients if they had to cease their operations due to lack of resources.

Private practice has experienced the opposite trend. Third-party financial involvement through increased insurance coverage and governmental subsidization has made services provided by private practitioners much more accessible. For example, in 1960 health care users paid almost half of the nation's medical expenditures out of their own pockets while government paid little more than 20 percent. In the last few years, direct payments by clients have accounted for only about a quarter of the nation's total health expenditures while government's share has gone up to 40 percent.[23] A substantial amount of these funds has been paid to private practitioners, including those in social work. With third-party financing, many more clients, including the economically disadvantaged, are availing themselves of a private practitioner's services. The clients believe that private services are more effective and less stigmatized than services through an agency. In addition, the private worker is often more available and geographically more accessible to them.[24]

Efficiency and cost-effectiveness are reasons accounting for these two opposite trends. It costs more to staff and equip a social agency than a private practitioner's office. One study of family service agencies indicated that interview costs exceeded the current rates charged by the local private practitioners.[25] In a study of a large and representative social agency, Gruber found that it took twelve dollars of income for the agency to provide one dollar's worth of direct service.[26] This occurs, he believes, because social agency systems are heavily staffed by administrative personnel who spend little, if any, time in actual service delivery, and the larger the agency, the more frequently this occurs. In agencies, only 29.5 percent of total staff time is spent seeing clients or providing colateral services. If a social worker in full-time private practice spent only 29.5 percent of his or her time doing this, the worker would be losing two-thirds of the income potential and would probably be in serious difficulty.

To stay in business, the practitioner must devote a much greater proportion of time to direct and colateral services. "Does this. . .explain why," Gruber asks, "the director of [a] family counseling agency could offer services through his private practice at a lower rate than his nonprofit agency could offer them?"[27]

Of course, it may be unfair to compare the cost-effectiveness of agency and private practice. Even though the differences are getting smaller, there are still significant differences in population served, in treatment modalities utilized, and in economic incentives operating in each.[28] Overhead will be less and direct service will be more in private work because there is more incentive to keep the hours filled. In public agencies, more time is presumably spent on improving the social conditions that lead to the problems as well as to proving unmeasurable and unchargeable services that only indirectly benefit the agencies' clients.

In any event, financially hard-pressed agency directors who have been seeking cost savings in service delivery are looking more carefully at private social work practice. Many of the private practitioner's methods are being emulated in agencies, and some agencies are contracting with private practitioners to provide agency services on a fee-for-service basis. Not only does this provide services for clients who otherwise might be placed on waiting lists, but, as Francis Turner pointed out, "agencies have found that productivity and effectiveness of private practitioners has been high and indeed an economical way of providing services."[29]

Notes and References

1. Theresa W. Barkan, "Private Casework Practice in a Medical Clinic," *Social Work,* 18 (July 1973), pp. 5–9.

2. National Association of Social Workers, "The NASW Code of Ethics," *Social Work,* 25 (May 1980), p. 185.

3. Irving Piliavin, "Restructuring the Provision of Social Services," *Social Work,* 13 (January 1968), pp. 34–41.

4. John Noll, "Needed—A Bill of Rights for Clients," *Professional Psychologist,* 5 (May 1974), pp. 3–12.

5. Francis Turner, *Psychosocial Therapy: A Social Work Perspective* (New York: Free Press, 1978), p. 178.

6. Ted B. Palmer, "Matching Worker and Client in Corrections," *Social Work,* 18 (March 1973), pp. 95–103.

7. Murray Bowen, *Family Therapy in Clinical Practice* (New York: Jason Aronson, 1978).

8. Robert Pruger, "The Good Bureaucrat," *Social Work,* 18 (July 1973), pp. 26–27.

9. Arnulf M. Pins, "Changes in Social Work Education and Their Implications for Practice," *Social Work,* 16 (April 1971), pp. 5–15.

10. Miriam Dinerman, *Social Work Curriculum at the Baccalaureate and Master's Levels* (New York: Lois & Samuel Silberman Fund, 1981), pp. 5–21.

11. Robert Constable, "New Directions in Social Work Education," *Journal of Education for Social Work,* 14 (Winter 1978), pp. 23–32.

12. Laura Epstein, "Is Autonomous Practice Possible?" *Social Work,* 18 (March 1973), pp. 5–12.

13. Herman Borenzweig, "Agency vs. Private Practice: Similarities and Differences," *Social Work,* 26 (May 1981), pp. 239–244.

14. Ruth R. Middleman, *A Study Guide for ACSW Certification* (Washington, D.C.: National Association of Social Workers, 1981).

15. National Association of Social Workers, "The NASW Code of Ethics," p. 184.

16. National Association of Social Workers, "Legislative Moves toward Licensure Continue Unabated," *NASW News,* 20 (September 1975), p. 12; and "States with Acts Regulating Social Work," *NASW News,* 29 (May 1984), p. 3.

17. David A. Hardcastle, "Public Regulation of Social Work," *Social Work,* 22 (January 1977), pp. 14–20.

18. Thomas L. Briggs, "A Critique of the NASW Manpower Statement," *Journal of Education for Social Work,* 10 (Winter 1975), p. 15.

19. "Standards for the Regulation of Social Work Practice," NASW Policy Statement No. 5 (Washington, D.C.: National Association of Social Workers, 1976), p. 3.

20. National Association of Social Workers, "Working Statement on the Purpose of Social Work," *Social Work,* 26 (January 1981), p. 6.

21. Borenzweig, "Agency vs. Private Practice," p. 243.

22. Richard Cloward and Frances Fox Piven, "Notes toward a Radical Social Work," in Roy Bailey and Mike Brake, eds., *Radical Social Work* (New York: Pantheon Books, 1975), p. vii.

23. Harry Schwartz, "Two Decades that Altered the Character of Medical Practice in America," *Medical Tribune,* 21 (May 7, 1980), p. 1.

24. Turner, *Psychosocial Therapy,* p. 179.

25. Scott Briar, "Family Services," in Henry S. Maas, ed., *Five Fields of Social Service: Reviews of Research* (New York: National Association of Social Workers, 1966), pp. 9–50.

26. Alan R. Gruber, "The High Cost of Delivering Services," *Social Work,* 18 (July 1973), pp. 33–40.

27. Ibid., p. 40.

28. Steven Sharfstein et al., "Problems in Analyzing the Comparative Costs of Private versus Public Psychiatric Care," *American Journal of Psychiatry,* 134 (January 1977), pp. 29–32.

29. Turner, *Psychosocial Therapy,* p. 178.

3

OCCUPATIONAL HAZARDS AND REWARDS

Many people, especially overworked and underpaid agency social workers, think private practice is a "bed of roses." They are right. It is often a nice place to be, but it is also full of thorns, bees, frost warnings, and manure.[1]

Why do social workers want to enter private practice? It is, after all, a venture filled with financial as well as professional risks. The rewards sought are never guaranteed and rarely as generous as anticipated. The hazards are guaranteed and are often more serious than expected.[2] Thus, the first thing a social worker who is thinking about going into private practice should do is objectively weigh the pros and cons, which sooner or later will have to be faced.

The private practitioner usually gives up a steady and secure job in a social agency and a predictable if not munificent income. Agency employment enables a worker to plan finances rationally, because income and professional costs are known. In private practice, income can fluctuate dramatically from month to month, while the expenses of maintaining an office are great, continuous, and seemingly always increasing. To enter private work, the practitioner gives up the relationship he or she had with fellow professionals at the agency, people with whom the burdens of caring for troubled clients could be shared. Private practice takes place in relative isolation, and the practitioner might go for hours or days seeing no one in the office but clients. The practitioner is at a disadvantage competing with members of other professions for the finite population of potential clients.[3] The public seems to know what the other helping professions do, what services they render, and what their qualifications are. Most people have much less understanding of what private social work practitioners do or what their particular expertise is.[4]

Many clients are hesitant about reimbursing the private social work practitioner. Many who are willing to pay expect the fee to be less than that for the services of other professionals. This impression is shared by insurance companies and other third-party financing institutions. Many of them will not help clients pay for social work services. Many of those that do help pay require the social worker to be supervised by a physician. When they are paid, social workers often are reimbursed at a much lower rate than are other helping professionals. Furthermore, third-party institutions often change requirements for payment and use what seem to be capricious criteria to determine whether and how much to pay social workers.

The private practitioner also contends with unpredictable variations in the national and local economies that influence the ability of clients to utilize the worker's services. The autonomous worker without an agency umbrella is directly accountable to the public and its regulating agencies, more vulnerable to the risks of malpractice, and under great pressure to maintain and demonstrate competence. The private practitioner devotes a considerable portion of time to the performance of the mundane but essential tasks of operating an independent business.[5] Such tasks can include typing letters, sending out bills, bookkeeping, confronting former clients about failure of payment, shopping for supplies, and cleaning and maintaining the office or finding someone to do it.

The private social worker rarely has a respite from clients, is on call twenty four hours daily, and must find some other professional person to cover every time a vacation or a day off to attend a professional meeting is taken. Because of their professional isolation and the public demands for accountability, private practitioners find it more important than ever to attend professional meetings and to take continuing education courses. However, time taken from the practice for such training reduces income. Yet, the practitioner usually finds it necessary to devote many hours and considerable energies to activities for which no income is received. For instance, the practitioner must give speeches to civic associations and offer consultation services to needy groups and relevant individuals. Such activities are important for gaining the necessary public exposure that can lead to more referrals and keep a practice viable.

Given such obstacles, why are thousands of social workers now entering private practice? No doubt a few take the plunge simply because they do not properly consider the problems they will encounter. Others become private practitioners not as a matter of choice but because other jobs are not available. (These days it is not easy for every social worker to get jobs in social agencies.) Thus, private practice might be viewed by some as a necessary evil, a temporary expedience to be tolerated until agency employment is found. Most of those who enter the field, however, do so by conscious choice after they have carefully weighed the advantages and disadvantages. For them, the potential benefits seem great enough to make their risk worth taking.

There are clearly many rewards available to the private practitioner who has the necessary motivation, luck, energy, and skill. For many, private practice represents the possibility of freedom from bureaucratic entanglements, a larger income, a greater challenge, and a better opportunity to serve the needs of clients. The autonomous social worker can by choice practice with clients directly for many years and never feel compelled, as does the experienced agency worker, to assume supervisory and administrative roles.[6] The private practitioner can create an autonomous working environment without having to accommodate the requirements of an agency or fellow personnel. Private practitioners can organize their offices in ways that best suit their values and professional specialties and can locate those offices in a neighborhood convenient for them and the clients they wish to serve. They can decide for themselves if they do or do not want to collaborate with anyone else, and they do not have to work with any other professional with whom they feel no compatibility. For many, private practice is the ideal way to be a social worker.

Is private or agency practice best? Obviously, there is no single, best career decision for everyone. Some workers will always be happier and more productive in agency settings; others will be better suited to private practice no matter how many problems they must face. Members of both groups can make a correct choice only if they are objective and realistic about it, if they consider the likely problems to be overcome, and if they learn how to minimize the difficulties before they actually enter private practice. Now that many social workers have been in private practice for a considerable length of time, there is a sizable literature about how to increase the chances of success.[7] The goal of this chapter, then, is to consolidate some of this information and describe the major hazards and rewards that social workers in private practice will encounter.

Four Hazards in Private Practice

Social workers in private practice or thinking about joining its ranks are most concerned about four major occupational hazards and obstacles to their success: the fear of financial problems, a concern about career difficulties, the possibility of malpractice suits, and public accountability.

The foremost of these concerns has to do with financial difficulties, and the economic uncertainties of private practice make this an understandable fear. No one wants to face indebtedness, bankruptcy, or destitution. Practitioners want to know in advance how much it will cost to operate a private office and business. They want to know what the anticipated revenues are likely to be. They want to have some way of knowing how to budget resources and avoid serious indebtedness if the hoped-for revenues are not forthcoming.

The second occupational hazard has to do with professional and career difficulties. These include such practical and inevitable problems as professional isolation, loneliness, burnout, lack of opportunity for promotion or other advancement, and the pressures of helping people while conducting a business. Most workers who consider private practice feel they will have no problem overcoming these factors, yet more private practitioners return to agency work for these than any other reasons.

The third problem area and one that most private practitioners prefer to avoid thinking about deals with malpractice. How likely is malpractice litigation for a private practitioner who works without supervision and who has no agency to divert some of the pressure? How important is it that the worker is ethical, competent, and practicing within the norms of the profession? Some helping professionals have lost malpractice suits even though their competence and practice was appropriate.

The fourth and final area of concern and risk has to do with professional and public accountability. Social work has lagged behind some of the other helping professions in the degree to which its private practitioners are regulated by and responsible to the public and to the consumers of their services. This is a serious problem for private practitioners because they must rely on their professional credentials rather than on agency or institutional employers to guarantee competence to the public.

All of these occupational hazards must be addressed and minimized by every social worker who hopes to have a durable private practice.

Minimizing Financial Problems

The risk of economic problems is usually the first and greatest worry facing anyone who contemplates private practice, and well it might be. A worker could easily spend thousands of dollars attempting to establish a practice before receiving one penny of income. The worker could borrow heavily to finance the high starting costs and then have to begin repaying the loan immediately. The practitioner has to be prepared to meet the monthly operating costs of a practice without any immediate assurance of enough clients and income to cover obligations, much less provide for living needs.

Starting Costs

Most full-time private practitioners find the costs of opening a practice roughly comparable to those of beginning lawyers and accountants self-employed in the same area. This is estimated to be a little more than half the annual salary a beginning social worker might make from agency employment. The starting costs usually include the first month's rent and two months' security deposit on the office lease, basic furniture and office equipment, carpeting, and necessary alterations to the office structure. Also included are costs for telephone installation, answering services or machines, printing office stationery, announcing the opening of the practice, getting malpractice and business insurance, and buying the multitude of inevitable incidentals that the individual worker will want or need. In chapter 5, there will be a discussion of the items to acquire for the typical private social work office. Obviously, the worker must walk a thin line between establishing an office that is spartan and frugal and one that is lavish. Going to extremes in either direction is not only inefficient in cost but can also dissuade potential clients from using the practitioner's services.

Reducing Starting Costs

Many social workers who enter private practice minimize the problem of initial expenses by renting space in the office of an existing psychotherapy practice. This usually means working in the office when the established professional is away unless there is extra space. This system enables the social worker to establish a clientele and to develop a source of income from private work before many expenses have to be met. Another option is to establish a private practice with other professionals so that many of the expenses can be shared or divided. However, the expenses of shared offices are never directly proportionate to the number of workers involved. In other words, it costs more than half a solo practitioner's starting costs apiece for two workers to open an office. Even so, the expenses are less than those borne by the worker who practices alone. Still another way to reduce starting costs is to lease furniture and office equipment rather than making outright purchases. There are two advantages: First, a considerable initial outlay does not have to be made, even though the monthly operating expenses will increase commensurate to the rental costs. Second, the practitioner is not stuck with the furniture and equipment if it is found that some items thought essential are not or that the particular practice requirements would have been better suited to another kind of furniture or office machine. Leasing makes experimentation and change possible. Also, leasing companies usually allow the customer to apply a portion of the rental costs toward purchase, so changing one's mind does not prove to be a costly lesson.

Another way to reduce starting costs is through the purchase of an existing practice. This possibility is rarely thought of as a way to reduce financial risks. Why pay someone a significant fee when it is possible to build one's own practice for free? Still, those who have done it point out advantages for the seller as well as the buyer.[8] The purchaser usually acquires the seller's office and all or most of the equipment, present clients, and records of past clients who may need more service. The seller also introduces and recommends the buyer to referral sources, writes letters of introduction to clients and community leaders, and, often, remains nearby as a consultant for a specified time. Typically, the price established is a percentage of the practice's average net receipts for the preceding three years or so. This sum is paid over a predetermined time as a percentage of the buyer's net receipts. Thus, if the purchaser earns little, the payment is little, and it is not all paid when the new practice is established. Of course, for this system to work, it is necessary that both buyer and seller have similar qualifications and interests, so that the clientele and referral base is transferable.

Monthly Operating Costs

The starting costs are, of course, just the beginning. To stay in private practice, the worker must make regular payments for the rent, telephone and utility bills, secretarial and maintenance services, office supplies, postage, continuing education expenses, and insurance. Most full-time workers calculate that between 20 and 30 percent of their gross incomes go for operating and overhead expenses if they maintain a full caseload. Some practitioners spend up to 50 percent of their gross receipts on overhead.[9] This percentage increases if the caseload is less than full. It decreases to some extent if the practice is shared with other practitioners. It also varies according to such individual circumstances as the amount of time a worker takes from practice because of illness, vacations, or education. Naturally, the operating expenses remain, even when the worker is not seeing clients.

Taxes and Retirement Funds

Other expenses that private practitioners must face are taxes and funds for retirement. Some private practitioners get into financial trouble because they are unable to set aside funds for these expenses. Unlike the worker employed in an institution, which withholds money for taxes and retirement without effort on the worker's part, the private practitioner must set aside, or save, money already received. It is easy, especially for the hard-pressed beginning worker, to postpone this savings program; one can omit paying for a retirement fund altogether, but it would be far better at the outset to get in the habit of setting aside something each month, no matter how small. (Various plans, including social security, insurance annuities, and Keogh plans, will be discussed in chapter 5.)

Setting aside funds for retirement may be optional, but income taxes for the federal and most state governments are not. The Internal Revenue Service requires *all* self-employed workers to make an estimate of their annual earnings, figure their taxes on these earnings, and make appropriate quarterly payments on these taxes. Failure to do so results in being closely scrutinized by the IRS thereafter, paying a fine for the amount not paid in the quarter, and, of course, paying the tax, too.[10] Many people who are self-employed find it difficult to set aside funds for this purpose, thinking that they will be able to make up the difference before the quarterly payment is due in January, April, June, and September. The social worker in private practice avoids difficulty by making a savings program for taxes a priority.

Estimating Earnings

Many social workers in private practice get into financial difficulty when they are not objective about the spendable income they receive from their practices. As the social worker begins to see many clients, it is easy to think that there is more money coming in than is the case. Because the practice seems financially successful, the practitioner may develop a more opulent lifestyle than is justified by spendable income. Experienced private practitioners have learned, sometimes the hard way, that vast wealth does not come even when many clients and high fees can be taken for granted.

Clients and agency-based social workers sometimes think private practitioners are wealthy because of the seemingly high fees charged. At first glance, it seems that the fee represents the practitioner's hourly pay, which some people multiply by the number of working hours in the week and year. Compared to the agency worker's pay, especially those funded by voluntary contributions or affiliated with religious organizations, the figure may seem very large indeed; however, the comparison of their salary with the hourly rate of the private practitioner is misleading.

It must be remembered that the private practitioner is only paid for *direct* services to clients, not for number of hours on the job. To keep a practice viable, the private practitioner must devote considerable time to activities that are not direct service and are thus without pay. No private practitioner could maintain the pace of seeing 40 clients a week, 52 weeks a year. Even if possible, it is unlikely that the worker would collect 100 percent billings, always keep a full schedule, and not have to take time away from the office for educational, administrative, or professional activities. When a private practitioner attends a professional conference, a criteria for maintaining professional competence, income stops. Vacations, consultations with other professionals, and bookkeeping are all done without reimbursement. The fee charged is often further diminished for reimbursement by insurance companies, who if they pay anything at all, do not cover the full amount of the charge. Almost all insurance companies have a cap on charges and require that providers not ask the client to pay above this limit; the companies generally enforce this provision by paying the provider nothing for subsequent services if the provision is not honored.

Insurance companies often refuse to reimburse for social work services unless the services are supervised by a physician. Many social workers in private practice deal with this requirement in an unsatisfactory way, but one that is seen as a necessary expedient: A physician, usually a psychiatrist, is paid a standard fee for regular meetings to act as a supervisor-consultant for the relevant cases. The physician then signs insurance forms and qualifying papers so that the social worker can be reimbursed.

Another factor to consider in estimating income is the social worker's involvement in indirect services. Unlike psychiatrists or psychologists, who typically retain some clinical detachment from the social and environmental issues facing most clients, the conscientious social worker is involved in such activities. Much valid social work occurs in the client's environment with friends, associations, fellow employees, and neighbors. If such activities are ignored, the social worker is engaging in a very narrow and limited version of the profession. With no agency to pay for such activity and little opportunity to charge the client for these indirect services, the worker's income is reduced commensurate to the time thus spent.

When all these factors are considered and deducted from what appears to be a high hourly fee, the private practitioner is not nearly as affluent as first imagined. If the practitioner shares an office or works part time, these finances have to be modified accordingly. Actually, it is difficult to find private social workers who are typical. Most full-time workers spend much more than forty hours weekly in their practice and most part-time workers in private practice are employed full time in an agency and then spend many additional hours in their private offices.

In spite of all the difficulties enumerated above, financial problems can be minimized by realistic thinking and objective planning. The private practitioner does not get into a good economic situation simply by showing up for work every day. Obviously, most private social workers receive good incomes and hold positive financial positions only with hard work, long hours, and a considerable amount of motivation.

Career Problems and How to Minimize Them

It is not uncommon for social workers to enter private practice, work long and hard, become firmly established and financially stabilized, and then give it all up to return to agency employment. They succeed in a business sense but still find that private work is not what they wanted or expected. What is missing for them? It is not that they are overwhelmed by obstacles or that they lack the resources to maintain private offices; they simply make conscious choices about the kind of work experiences they want and come to believe that private practice does not offer it to them. They experience the special career problems inherent in private practice: professional isolation, burnout, boredom, stress, low prestige, and having to work with clients and referral sources who are outside their range of interests. Of course, these problems are by no means the exclusive province of the private practitioner, but the private worker often chooses this type of work to get away from such problems. If the worker has to endure the risks and pressures of private practice without getting away from such problems, the job can quickly lose its appeal.

Professional Isolation

One characteristic of the private practice job to which workers have great difficulty adapting is its isolation. Agency workers have frequent opportunities for informal exchanges with their colleagues, but private practitioners do not. Even when the private worker shares an office with other professionals, there is little opportunity for such exchanges. Private social workers are kept busy seeing clients, contacting referral sources, or managing the business aspects of the practice; there is little time or inclination for fraternizing with peers, and the worker often feels alone and detached. Yet, any worker needs to share the worries, to ventilate frustrations about jobs and clients, and to get away from constantly performing a professional role. Feedback from one's peers, supportive relationships from colleagues, time away from the workday, and work sharing, have been shown to be more important to social work job satisfaction than higher pay or variety.[11] The private worker can easily become emotionally depleted if there is only a one-way flow of emotions from worker to client; there is a clear need for a two-way flow of feelings, and this can best come through closer collegial and peer relationships.

A sense of isolation is a particularly serious problem for the worker who hangs out a shingle at a relatively early age and continues in private work for many years. Agency workers often change jobs or move within an agency to different roles during the course of their careers. The private worker, however, does essentially the same job throughout his or her career. The only chance for variety is to return to agency practice or to change professions.

Burnout

For some, professional isolation leads to the serious malady known as "burnout."[12] This is a form of depression and apathy and is related to boredom, intellectual stagnation, and nonmotivation for effective client service. Agency-based social workers are certainly afflicted with this condition in great numbers because of difficult working conditions and frustrations.[13] The private worker is equally vulnerable and has less opportunity to prevent and recuperate from it. The private worker may not even be aware of burnout symptoms unless in contact with peers. No one is there to point out that it is happening or to encourage the worker to take corrective measures before it gets worse. Problems of this type can best be prevented when the social worker maintains close contacts with other social workers, keeps intellectually stimulated, and grows in knowledge and skill. The danger for the private practitioner is that it is so easy to put off taking the necessary steps and so easy to let burnout creep in without suspecting its presence. The safeguard is to assume its inevitability unless opportunities for collegial relationships are built into the way practice is maintained.

Stress

Professionals frequently leave private practice because of the stress of the job. Employees in agencies work forty hours or less each week and are able to leave many of their concerns at the office when they are done for the day. Other workers cover for them in their absence; they can focus their attention on serving clients rather than on worrying about self-promotion and office management. Private practitioners, however, usually work much more than forty hours per week, often on weekends and evenings; clients frequently have access to them at all hours. Practitioners are subjected to the pressures of single-handedly meeting office expenses and dealing with the myriad of details inherent in running a business. Such stress often takes a physical and emotional toll.[14] If the practitioner works elsewhere part time, the stress can be even greater; spending forty hours in an agency and then several hours each evening and all day Saturdays in private practice is a typical pattern, and it can be a dangerous burden if precautions are not taken. Full-time and part-time private practitioners who remain healthy mitigate such problems by pacing themselves so they can have respites and by maintaining good professional and personal relationships. It helps to take long lunch hours or have physical activities in the middle of the workday. Meeting with colleagues in agencies for intellectual stimulation is important, as are regular vacations and frequent variations in the working routine.

Professional Esteem

One career problem that many agency workers would find hard to understand concerns the worker's lack of recognition for professionalism. Private practice is sometimes seen by other social workers as among the most prestigious of the direct practice activities. Why, then, would a private practitioner feel any problem about this? It is because status and prestige are relative; professionals are accorded recognition for their expertise by "relevant others." For agency workers, this means clients and other social workers. They meet with other professionals as representatives of the agency rather than as representatives of the profession. The private worker's relevant others are more likely to be members of professions outside social work—physicians, lawyers, judges, and other officials. In such circumstances, social work is frequently not given much recognition for credibility or expertise. A private practitioner must often spend inordinate amounts of time explaining the nature of the profession and its particular expertise. Skeptical insurance companies, potential clients, and referral sources must all be educated as to the private worker's knowledge, abilities, and professional credibility. This does not usually provide a feeling that private workers are held in high regard by others.

Clients

Another career problem for private practitioners is the type of clients with whom they deal. In many ways, private practitioners have an advantage over agency workers in this regard because clients are more highly motivated and thus are more cooperative and workable.[15] Most private practitioners, however, are not as selective of their clients as they should be; they often take whatever clients come their way. Thus, if they are less equipped to work with certain kinds of clients or client problems, they will have less than optimal outcomes. If they worked in agencies, where clients are screened and sent to them because of their special skills, this problem is less pronounced. In private work, the practitioner can minimize this risk for themselves as well as the client by being objective about their own skills and interests, by being selective about the clients they will accept for service, and by referring clients to professionals who are more qualified. This will help prevent frustration and is crucial in minimizing the risks of malpractice.

Avoiding Malpractice Litigation

Malpractice is the third major occupational hazard faced by private practitioners. It is a concern becoming prevalent among professionals in this increasingly litigious society. Not long ago, a social worker was sued for malpractice.[16] Everyone knew she was a capable, well-qualified professional, a dedicated person who could be relied on by her clients and fellow employees. Ironically, her troubles began because she was so highly regarded. Her job was helping in the evaluation of people who were hospitalized with emotional disturbances. Prompt decisions about them were required by law: Should they be retained voluntarily, released to outpatient treatment, or committed? These questions needed rapid answers for every admission. Usually, the worker interviewed the client and family members before preparing reports. The reports were used by judges and court-designated psychiatrists who made the final decision. One day the worker interviewed a young man and his family. Her resulting report suggested that he was not likely to be dangerous. The psychiatrist in charge had no time to give an intensive examination to the young man before the case had to go before the judge, so, based on the report, he recommended discharge. Soon after the man was released, he shot several people and then himself.

Eventually, the victims and their families sued both the psychiatrist and the social worker for malpractice: the doctor for the improper recommendation and the social worker for providing the information that led to it. The malpractice suit took years to resolve; it would have taken longer except that the defendants finally agreed to settle out of court. They agreed to pay the plaintiffs over $60,000, a sum that did not cover the extensive court costs and attorney fees. The social worker had not wanted to settle, but pressure was intense. Her codefendant wanted to settle to avoid further negative publicity and wanted her to do likewise. She faced substantial legal expenses, and the time she spent in courtrooms and law offices was deducted from her salary. The incessant questioning of her professional competence was taking a stressful, painful toll. Ultimately, she felt she had little choice but to settle despite her continued assertion and belief that she had committed no wrong.

Litigation Worries

Because private practitioners have less protection from litigation than practitioners in agencies, they might have more cause for worry than their agency-based counterparts. The private practitioner has less professional supervision, no other workers with whom to share the burden or blame for problems, and little help from other professionals in making the many professional decisions regarding clients' well-being. Agencies sometimes diffuse the focus of attention from an individual worker in a possible malpractice incident, and they often assume some of the responsibility for the problem.

Litigation can happen to any social worker, inside or outside agency auspices. It can happen to anyone, no matter what their level of skill or quality of their work. There are no fail-safe formulas that guarantee against malpractice suits. Among other reasons, it happens because the laws and standards pertaining to professional practice, especially in the private sector, are inconsistent and have been interpreted unpredictably.[17] Some helping professionals, for example, have been sued for confining patients in institutions. Others have been sued for not confining patients in institutions (as in the example given above). Sometimes, professionals have lost court actions for not breaking confidentiality and failing to warn people who might be endangered by the client. Other practitioners have been sued for divulging confidences. Many suits have occurred over the issue of incorrect diagnosis; others have been filed for devoting excessive and costly resources to diagnostic testing at the expense of treatment. The list of reasons for malpractice liability is endless, and the public predisposition to sue is now being accompanied by an oversupply of underemployed lawyers who take cases on contingency. It is little wonder that workers worry about being sued for malpractice.

Malpractice Probabilities

There are some comforting facts to consider. Social workers are still less likely to be sued than most other professionals in private practice. In fact, the insurance underwriter for most social work malpractice policies indicates that there have been few successful malpractice suits brought against social workers.[18] Most litigation is against professionals who provide physical care for their patients.[19] For example, among all U.S. physicians, one malpractice suit is initiated for every seven years of practice. This varies according to specialty. Those medical specialists who have less involvement with the patients' physical care are far less likely to be sued. As a group, psychiatrists are sued only once for every 50 to 100 years of practice. Most of the litigation that has taken place against them centers around inappropriate dispensations of medication or orders for a patient to be confined. Social workers have little to do with these aspects of health care, so they are less likely than psychiatrists to be involved in suits.

For those who do get sued, the prognosis is not as grim as some might expect. Of all the malpractice suits against professionals in the United States, only 6.5 percent ever reach a verdict.[20] Most of the verdicts have favored the defendant, and those that go against the professional are usually for endurable amounts. Almost 60 percent of the claims are for less than $3,000, and 95 percent of the judgments are for amounts well under $40,000. When only cases that exclude physical care are considered, the amounts are lower still. Heretofore, the highest judgment against a professional who was not involved in the physical care of a client was made in 1973, when a psychologist was ordered to pay $170,000 in damages.[21] The highest settlement against a social worker to date has been $60,000, and this is a highly unusual circumstance.

Unfortunately, such reassuring statistics will not remain valid for social workers indefinitely. As their numbers in private practice increase and as their public visibility becomes more pronounced, the chances of malpractice suits will grow. Private practitioners have not been sued that often partly because they have not been noticed. Another reason is that their traditional clients have tended to be the more disadvantaged and powerless people who have not been inclined or able to engage in legal controversy. As they work with more affluent clients, ones who have more power and predisposition toward litigation, vulnerability increases. As they take responsibility for more complex treatment methods outside institutional auspices, the risk mounts further. They can no longer rely on comfortable statistics. Now their best hope is a clear understanding of the behaviors that lead to such problems and an ability to avoid such activities whenever possible.

Causes of Litigation

What behaviors are most likely to result in malpractice litigation? The worker can be required to pay damages if it can be shown that failure to live up to a specified standard of professional behavior caused the client direct or proximate damage. Usually, expert testimony by other social workers is required to tell the court if the conduct met the standards of the profession.[22]

Standards of conduct encompass an infinite variety of possible behaviors that may or may not be appropriate for a given situation. The standards of conduct are not only determined by one's profession but are also defined by the laws of the states in which the incident occurred and by the norms regarding any business transaction or other human interaction. Nevertheless, it is possible to single out a few of the infinite variety of behaviors that have most frequently led professionals into litigation. These include problems about (1) informed consent, (2) faulty diagnosis and resulting treatment, (3) physical restraint and bodily harm, (4) confidentiality and defamation, (5) failure to warn those threatened by clients, (6) limitations of ability to perform a needed service and failure to refer to a professional with the needed ability, (7) misuse of therapy, and (8) inappropriate termination and abandonment of the client.

Informed Consent. When one of the above behaviors leads a plaintiff to take action, the issue of informed consent is likely to become part of the argument.[23] Clients must willingly and explicitly consent to any treatment they are offered. Only when the client is institutionalized, a minor, or judged incompetent to make decisions is there an exception. Even then, consent must be obtained from the person legally responsible. The private practitioner is unlikely to have trouble about consent because clients come of their own volition. This is a tangible indication that consent has taken place. There is, however, the risk that the client was not sufficiently informed to give sound consent. In one case, a couple sought marital therapy from a private practitioner and they were not informed that divorce could be an outcome of treatment. In treatment, they came to understand that their marriage was surviving largely because of their feelings of insecurity and fear of the economic consequences. The treatment was successful in enhancing their ego strengths and restoring their self-confidence, and one of the partners eventually sought a divorce. The other felt the action was the result of the marital therapy and sued the therapist. The case was not won by the litigant, but the therapist had to defend herself against the action.[24]

Several court cases have clearly determined and re-enforced the principle that any professional who offers treatment is obliged to warn the client of potential adverse effects or dangers that can come from the treatment. It is therefore in the interests of the practitioner and the client that the risks inherent in the therapy relationship be made clear and explicit before there is an agreement to begin work.

Faulty Diagnosis and Inappropriate Treatment. Private practitioners are at risk in providing treatment that is based on a faulty diagnosis. The greatest area of vulnerability is in treating someone who has apparently psychogenic symptoms, which turn out to be organic. Private workers who do not recommend clients to get complete physical examinations before beginning treatment are exposing themselves and their clients to needless risks. The other vulnerability is in improper incarceration. Usually, social workers do not make diagnoses that lead to incarceration, but they can have problems by providing information that leads to improper confinement.[25] Conversely, if the information results in releasing a dangerous client, as shown earlier, there is risk of malpractice. If information provided to others by the worker is faulty and leads to incorrect conclusions, the social worker shares the responsibility.

Bodily Harm. Social workers rarely need to worry about the risk of bodily harm to their clients because they have little to do with the physical aspects of their care. Bodily harm is most likely to occur when the social worker uses therapy techniques that lead to clients being physically hurt. This has happened in active group therapy and in encounter sessions in which some clients are encouraged to vent their feelings physically. If a client is injured as a result of these activities, there is some possibility of litigation, but this possibility can be minimized with informed consent and proper precautions that prevent the situation from getting too rough.

Confidentiality and Defamation. Social workers are justifiably proud of their consistent adherence to ethical principles, so they may have little fear about the confidentiality risk. The NASW Code of Ethics explicitly forbids violations of this standard, so if it occurred, there would be no question in court of whether the behavior conformed to professional standards.[26] However, there are some instances where maintaining confidentiality can lead to legal difficulties.[27] In the famous *Yoder* v. *Smith* case, a physician was sued when he informed the patient's employer of some medical problems that prevented the patient from continuing to do his job. The doctor was asked by the patient to provide this information, and the patient later realized the disclosure was harmful.[28]

Sometimes the practitioner is forced to walk a fine line between violating a law or violating this ethical principle.[29] For example, many states now legally compel professionals to inform authorities if their clients are suspected of committing child or spouse abuse. Any worker upholding this law is vulnerable to litigation on the basis of defamation if the client has not harmed the family member. If the law requires this of social workers and other professionals, the practitioner must so inform the client.

Duty to Warn. Closely related to confidentiality and defamation problems is the requirement in many states to warn potential victims whenever a client makes threats in the practitioner's hearing. This requirement was imposed retroactively when it was first instituted in California in the 1975 *Tarasoff* decision.[30] In this case, a student at the University of California, Berkeley, was in treatment in the campus mental health clinic. He told the therapist of his plan to kill a young woman, Tatiana Tarasoff, because she broke off her relationship with him. The therapist and his supervisor took the threat seriously, informed the campus police, and the young man was detained. However, the man convinced the authorities that he was harmless. Soon after the police release the man, he murdered the woman. Her family sued the therapist and the university for failing to warn them of her peril. Eventually, the State Supreme Court upheld the decision that the therapist should have warned them. This interpretation now has the force of law in California and many other states. Such an interpretation could be made in any jurisdiction in the United States and thus puts the practitioner in an impossible dilemma. If the social worker warns someone everytime a client makes a threat, the client would be justified in suing the worker for defamation if no harm was actually done. Yet if the worker did not issue the warning and the threat was carried out, there would be the possibility of litigation.

What can the practitioner do to resolve such a dilemma? None of the possibilities are completely satisfactory. Psychiatrists Roth and Meisel researched the issue and made several recommendations for all therapists.[31] First, they say, the practitioner should not issue warnings unless the client's dangerousness is unequivocally certain. Threats are seldom carried out, and workers can always be more helpful to such clients if the working relationship is maintained. The worker must, however, inform the client that the confidentiality provision has exceptions, including threats to others. Second, if the client still seems intent on harming someone, the social worker may tell the client what the law requires the worker to do if the threats persist. Third, a social worker can sometimes use environmental modification to vitiate a client's dangerousness. For example, the worker might convince the client to get rid of any weapons or call upon the client's family for support in looking after the client. Finally, if the worker has no choice but to warn the potential victim, the worker should first inform the client of the intent and if possible obtain permission to divulge the information. The worker should also attempt to reveal the information to the intended victim in the client's presence. Obviously, these measures are not completely satisfactory to the worker and are not likely to delight the client. However, they are an expedience. The worker must above all consider the effect on the client and weigh the odds.

Limitations on Ability. Another source of malpractice litigation takes place when the client needs some type of treatment that the professional is not qualified to provide. Suits arising from this problem are rare for social workers who deal with emotional problems but more common for professionals who provide physical treatments. Nurses, physical therapists, chiropractors, optometrists, and similar occupational groups have faced suits for providing treatments that have been declared the province of physicians. If the social worker provides treatment outside a recognized realm of expertise and, in doing so, keeps the client from going to the appropriate professional, malpractice actions can be justified. The social worker is required to inform the client of his or her limitations in providing needed services and must always refer the client to the appropriate other professional, if it seems necessary.

Misuse of Therapy. Some professionals have been sued because they took advantage of the therapy relationship for their own purposes. There have been many court judgments against professionals who have engaged in sexual relationships with their clients or who have influenced clients to give them large sums of money.[32] If the relationship between worker and client is effective, the client will develop trust and confidence in the worker. The feeling might be based on transference or simply due to conscious appreciation of the worker's ability and concern. Whatever the origins of the feeling, the worker is often in a position to misuse the therapy. Such conduct is clearly and explicitly beyond appropriate standards for social workers. The NASW Code of Ethics states that "social workers should under no circumstances engage in sexual activities with clients."[33] The Code also indicates that activities benefiting the worker to the detriment of the client are unethical. The precaution here is obvious. Private practitioners should avoid any relationship with the client except that which is clearly therapeutic and within the ethical principles of the profession.

Premature Termination or Abandonment. The last important behavior that leads to malpractice incidents involves prematurely ending treatment when the need for it remains. Private practitioners are often accused of not seeing clients whose funds or insurance runs out. Most professions, including social work, recognize that it is unethical to end treatment when the need continues, regardless of the client's financial circumstance. There must be an orderly and professionally prescribed process of termination. Treatment ends only when both worker and client agree to conclude, or when the client unilaterally decides to end it. Usually, it is wise to put the decision to terminate in writing.

One variation of this problem is what lawyers call abandonment. Suits have been made against professionals who have taken extended vacations without properly assuring the continued care of their clients. Agency-based workers are at less risk in such situations because the client can go to other staff members if needed. The private social worker has no similar option. The worker must have another professional cover, should always inform clients of any planned absence and should make all relevant information about the client available to the covering professional. The practitioner would do well to establish a working relationship with one or two other professionals so they can cover for one another. Of course, the worker is vulnerable unless accurate records about the client are provided for the professional who is covering. If the covering worker cannot continue with treatment because existing information is unavailable, a client who is harmed could be justified in seeking redress.

There are, of course, many other behaviors that could lead a private practitioner into malpractice actions, but those discussed are the most worrisome and prevalent. Because the laws seem inconsistent or are interpreted inconsistently, there can be no certainty of avoiding malpractice problems. The worker's recourse is to reduce the odds by adhering strictly to the manifest standards of the profession and to the publicly sanctioned norms applying to all professional conduct. Yet, if every professional always played it safe, always conformed to existing treatment procedures, and never ventured forth into unexplored realms, there is no doubt that creativity and progress would be diminished.

Accountability and Quality Assurance Problems

The last of the major occupational hazards in private practice has to do with demonstrating competence to the consumer and to one's professional peers. Traditionally, social work's clients did not put their trust in the worker or the worker's profession, but in the agency where the service was provided. The worker's credibility came from the reputation of the agency and its staff. This has been dramatically changing in the past few years. Third-party funding organizations as well as the clients themselves are starting to insist that the providers and workers rather than the agencies be held accountable for their actions.[34] Nowadays, all professionals, whether in fee-for-service arrangements or salaried in social agencies, are participating in quality control efforts such as competency testing, peer review, licensing and certification, and continuing education. Private practitioners in social work have been at the forefront of their profession's effort to upgrade these programs. This is probably not done altruistically but because their ability to compete with the other professions depends on it. Insurance companies are understandably unwilling to pay for the services of any professional group that cannot demonstrate its competence. Clients are less willing to partake of the services of any such group. Private practitioners would have no way of maintaining their reputations if their ranks could be entered by anyone, regardless of abilities.

Social work has fallen behind many of the other professions in these programs. Most of the other mental health professionals in private practice are licensed in every state. The professions have rigorous tests of competence for all their members; they require a certain amount of continuing education for each member to keep the person current with directions in the field, and they keep records to assure that each member has done so. Social work is taking steps to catch up.[35] At this time, a social worker need not pass a competency exam to be recognized as a member of the profession. One need not be an ACSW to be a social worker. No social worker has to prove he or she has kept current, except in the few states where this is required. Instead, the worker is expected to continue education on his or her own and to use the honor system to keep track of credits.

No doubt, all this is due to the social work tradition of deriving credibility from agency rather than professional auspices. It is also due to the difficulty the profession has had in carving out a unique "turf," which is usually a prerequisite of licensing.[36] Whatever the reason, it will constitute a hardship on private practitioners and their clients until such programs are further upgraded. The private social worker has a difficult time showing potential clients, referral sources, and third-party financing institutions qualifications in the desired skills. If the worker is highly trained, capable of passing any examination, has kept current with innovations in the profession, and is willing to endure professional review, there is still little systematic way of doing so in most states. This crucial issue of qualifications is discussed further in chapter 4.

Rewards of Private Practice

Given the assortment of obstacles and hazards facing the private practitioner, one wonders why anyone would have the incentive to seek entry into the field. What is the motivation? Despite the obstacles, there are many desirable aspects to private work. Social workers are hanging out their shingles because the rewards are considerable.

The motivations for entering and remaining in private practice include the opportunity to perform professional services independently, without supervision or agency constraints; determination of one's own work habits and schedules; flexibility; the chance to remain in direct practice with clients; the opportunity to earn more money, face more challenges, and gain more recognition and prestige; and the opportunity to work with well-motivated clients.[37] As previously discussed, some of these motivations are illusory, but they remain the perceived, if not the actual, rewards of private social work practice. Some elaboration of each follows.

Freedom from Bureaucracy

Social workers, as well as members of other professions, consistently report that they appreciate the freedom from organizational constraints as the most powerful incentive for private practice. Social workers, like all professionals, devote a considerable part of their lives to acquiring skills, knowledge, and experience to serve their clients effectively. Many of them feel that social agency work prevents them from utilizing these skills. Agencies, like all bureaucracies, have established work rules, lines of authority, supervision requirements, and many other controls on their employees. The system is, of course, necessary and worthwhile for the agency, but it prevents the individual worker from making independent decisions. The private practitioner has more flexibility and opportunity to exercise professional judgments.

Flexibility in Work

The private practitioner maintains a work schedule based on need, interests, and lifestyle. The practitioner sets a personal pace, defines what hours to work, and decides independently when to take time away from the office. The practitioner can decide what professional meetings to attend and when to attend them. The agency worker, however, must conform to a predetermined work schedule and timetable. This is necessary so that the agency activity is coordinated and the agency provided with adequate staff coverage. The idea of greater freedom for the private practitioner, however, is usually more theoretical than practical. Most experienced private practitioners find themselves tied to their offices with little flexibility about their hours; they tend to demand much more of themselves than they would tolerate from a supervisor in an agency, and they do this of their own volition. However, whether they use their freedom or not, it is there and it is priceless.

Remaining in Direct Practice

In social agencies, it is typical for workers to be promoted to supervisory and administrative responsibilities. When this happens, the worker often becomes too busy for direct practice and no longer does the job for which she or he was trained and originally motivated. Not accepting the job change may mean eventually coming under the authority of workers who have had much less experience, and income and credibility among peers remain static. Unless the worker wants to assume supervisory and administrative responsibilities, private practice is the most reasonable alternative. The worker can continue to work directly with clients, and income and approbation remain commensurate with skills.

Financial Considerations

Even though the difference between agency and private practice spendable income is not as great as expected, the financial rewards of the latter can be considerable. Agencies are limited in how much they can pay their workers, no matter how motivated, skillful, and hardworking the agency worker is. The financial reward of the private worker, however, will be commensurate with skill and effort. Effective private social workers are in the top earning brackets of their profession and earn about as much as most other nonmedical mental health professionals.

Challenge

Another motivation for many social workers is the challenge of private practice. Many workers want to test their limits without organizational constraints, to see if they can manage a business as well as perform a professional role competently. They appreciate being responsible primarily to themselves. They know the risks are there, and they want to see if they can overcome them. They want to put into practice what they believe to be professional work and to serve clients based on their own knowledge rather than on the requirements of an employer.

Motivated Clients

Finally, many enter private social work practice because they want to work with clients who are motivated. Agency workers often say they are frustrated in their attempts to provide services for clients who are undoubtedly in need but who lack the incentive or interest to do much about their difficulty. Agencies such as prisons, hospitals, public assistance offices, and juvenile courts often deal with clients who are forced to accept the worker's help whether they want it or not. In such cases, both the client and worker often simply go through the motions of the contact so that both will be conforming to the requirements of the agency. The worker must spend a disproportionate amount of time filling out forms and acting as an agent of social control. Many social workers go into private practice because it is an avenue away from such experience. Of course, they are then not working with the most disadvantaged and needy in order to provide services for those who may have less need. This motive is not one in which private practitioners should feel pride, however; it is the antithesis of the fundamental value base of the profession and an elitist behavior at that. It is, however, clearly a reason some social workers have for entering private practice, and it should not be ignored.

These incentives are not automatic for all who enter and remain in private practice. They exist for most of those who work hard, are knowledgeable, skillful, and lucky. The worker who still wants to enter private practice after weighing all the pros and cons must determine if the qualifications and personal attributes to make success possible are in hand.

Notes and References

1. Herbert Roth, "Independent Practice," *Family Therapy News*, 14 (May 1983), p. 8.

2. Herbert Freudenberger, "Hazards of Psychotherapeutic Practice," *Psychotherapy in Private Practice*, 1 (Spring 1983), pp. 83–91.

3. Robert Barker, "Supply Side Economics in Private Psychotherapy Practice: Some Ominous and Encouraging Trends," *Psychotherapy in Private Practice*, 1 (Spring 1983), pp. 71–82.

4. Willard G. Richan and Allan R. Mendelsohn, *Social Work: The Unloved Profession* (New York: Franklin Watts, 1973), pp. 18–31.

5. C. H. Browning, *Private Practice Handbook: The Tools and Techniques for Successful Practice Development* (2d ed.; Los Alamitos, Calif.: Duncliffs, 1982), p. 18.

6. Raymond Monsour Scurfield, "Clinician to Administrator: Difficult Role Transition?" *Social Work*, 26 (November 1981), pp. 495–501.

7. Robert L. Barker, *The Business of Psychotherapy: Private Practice Administration for Therapists, Counselors, and Social Workers* (New York: Columbia University Press, 1982); Browning, *Private Practice Handbook;* J. R. Cookerly and K. McClaren, *How to Increase Your Private Practice Power* (Ft. Worth, Tex.: Center for Counseling & Developmental Services, 1982); D. E. Hendrickson, S. P. Janney, and J. E. Fraze, *How to Establish Your Own Private Practice* (Muncie, Ind.: Contemporary Press, 1978); James Kilgore, "Establishing and Maintaining a Private Practice," *Journal of Marriage and Family Counseling*, 1 (April 1975), pp. 145–148; Arnold Levin, *Psychotherapy Private Practice* (New York: Free Press, 1983); Mark H. Lewin, *Establishing and Maintaining a Successful Professional Practice* (Rochester, N.Y.: Professional Development Institute, 1978); and Louis Mone, *Private Practice: A Professional Business* (La Jolla, Calif.: Elm Press, 1983). See also the journals, *Psychotherapy in Private Practice* and *Psychotherapy Finances*.

8. Robert Weitz, "I Sold My Private Practice," pp. 101–104, and Richard Samuels, "I Bought His Private Practice," pp. 105–108, *Psychotherapy in Private Practice*, 1 (Spring 1983).

9. Roth, "Independent Practice," p. 8.

10. Sheldon Gorlick, "Tax Audits: How to Dodge the IRS Bullet," *Medical Economics,* January 24, 1983, pp. 171–174.

11. Ayala Pines and Ditsa Kafry, "Occupational Tedium in the Social Services," *Social Work,* 23 (November 1978), pp. 499–507.

12. Herbert Freudenberger and Geraldine Richelson, *Burnout: The High Cost of Achievement* (New York: Doubleday, Anchor Press, 1980), pp. 73–78.

13. Martha Bramhall and Susan Ezell, "How Burned Out Are You?" *Public Welfare,* 39 (Winter 1981), pp. 23–27.

14. Barry Farber and Louis Heifetz, "The Satisfaction and Stresses of Psychotherapeutic Work: A Factor Analytic Study," *Professional Psychiatry,* 12 (May 1981), pp. 621–628.

15. George W. Ayers et al., "Fees in a Human Service Agency: Why Do Clients Pay?" *Social Work,* 26 (May 1981), pp. 245–248.

16. Barker, *The Business of Psychotherapy,* p. 215.

17. Ralph Slovenko, *Psychiatry and Law* (Boston: Little, Brown & Co., 1973).

18. Correspondence with American Professional Agency, Amityville, N.Y., March 18, 1983.

19. U.S. Department of Health and Human Services, *Medical Malpractice: Report of the Secretary's Commission on Malpractice* (Washington, D.C.: U.S. Government Printing Office, 1981), pp. 2–4.

20. Chester Trent and William Muhl, "Professional Liability Insurance and the American Psychiatrist," *American Journal of Psychiatry,* 132 (December 1975), pp. 1312–1315.

21. Ronald K. Green and Gibbi Cox, "Social Work and Malpractice: A Converging Course," *Social Work,* 23 (March 1978), pp. 100–105; and Beatrix Shear, *The Malpractice Problem for Non-Physician Health Care Professionals as Reflected in Professional Liability Rates,* Publication No. 573-88 (Washington, D.C.: U.S. Department of Health, Education & Welfare, 1973), p. 14.

22. Barton E. Bernstein, "Malpractice: An Ogre on the Horizon," *Social Work,* 23 (March 1978), pp. 106–112.

23. John Noll, "The Psychotherapist and Informed Consent," *American Journal of Psychiatry,* 133 (December 1976), pp. 1451–1453.

24. Robert Barker, *Treating Couples in Crisis: Theory and Practice in Marital Therapy* (New York: Free Press, 1984), pp. 204–206.

25. Frank M. Johnson, Jr., "Court Decisions and the Social Services," *Social Work,* 20 (September 1975), pp. 343–347.

26. National Association of Social Workers, "The NASW Code of Ethics," *Social Work,* 25 (May 1980), p. 186, as cited in Elizabeth Howe, "Public Professions and the Private Model of Professionalism."

27. Barton E. Bernstein, "Privileged Communications to the Social Worker," *Social Work,* 22 (July 1977), pp. 264–268.

28. Slovenko, *Psychiatry and Law,* p. 243.

29. See, for example, "45 Landmark Decisions," *Family Therapy News,* 14 (May 1983), p. 8. (Reprinted from *Family Advocate,* 5 [Summer 1982], pp. 4–5.)

30. Tarasoff v. Regents of the University of California, 14, 551, P2d, 334 (1976); and Robert L. Barker, "The Tarasoff Paradox: Confidentiality and the Duty to Warn," *Social Thought,* 10 (to be published 1984).

31. Loren Roth and Alan Meisel, "Dangerousness, Confidentiality, and the Duty to Warn," *American Journal of Psychiatry,* 134 (May 1977), pp. 508–511.

32. Dorothy Tennov, *Psychotherapy: The Hazardous Cure* (New York: Doubleday/Anchor Press, 1978.)

33. National Association of Social Workers, "The NASW Code of Ethics," p. 185.

34. Irene Oppenheimer, "Third-Party Payments," *Social Policy,* 8 (November–December 1977), pp. 55–58.

35. National Association of Social Workers, "Regulatory Bills See Light of Day," *NASW News,* 28 (May 1983), p. 13.

36. David A. Hardcastle, "Public Regulation of Social Work," *Social Work,* 22 (January 1977), p. 15.

37. Barker, *The Business of Psychotherapy,* pp. 74–78.

4

GETTING AND STAYING QUALIFIED

Not long ago, a social worker decided to go into private practice. She had given careful thought to its potential hazards and rewards and believed it would be worth the risk. After all, she thought, she had all the right qualifications. She had several advanced degrees from accredited schools of social work. She had years of agency experience under good supervision. She had always been held in high regard by her colleagues, clients, and agency employers. She was professionally certified and she had kept her knowledge up to date through many continuing education courses and professional seminars. As to her personal attributes for succeeding in the venture, she knew there would be no problem. She was a hard worker and could work independently. She had the financial resources to support a practice until it could become self-sustaining. Even the setting for her practice seemed ideal. She planned to establish it in her home, where there was an office that was directly accessible to the street. Her home was in a comfortable, upper middle-class neighborhood, and a physician and a dentist had their practices in similar houses nearby. And so, with little fanfare, she placed a tiny sign on which was her name, degree, and profession in the office window. She was now in private practice. How could she go wrong?

She found out very soon. Within weeks she was in a courtroom, defending herself against charges of breaking the law. She was accused of violating a county zoning ordinance that said only members of *"recognized* professions" could operate practices in home offices (author's emphasis). "Only recognized professionals?" she thought when the authorities notified her. "Then what does the county consider me to be—a fortune teller?"

In fact, the zoning statute had been instituted to protect the residents of the neighborhood from fortune tellers and others whose work was perceived as disruptive to the character of the neighborhood. However, because the ruling said no one except members of "recognized professions," the issue quickly became a question of whether or not social work was a recognized profession. If the worker could prove that it was, she could continue her private practice. If she could not, she would have to close her new office.

The National Association of Social Workers, her professional association, helped in her defense because it appeared that the whole profession was on trial.[1] Witnesses were called by both sides to show why social work was or was not a recognized profession. The issue took many weeks to resolve, and the outcome was equivocal. The county ultimately avoided saying that social work was not a recognized profession. Instead, it reworded its zoning ordinances. Thereafter, no one, regardless of affiliation or qualification, could operate a home office without prior county approval. The worker was permitted to keep her private practice, but the costly legal defense meant her office was already thousands of dollars in the red.

Many social workers have had to learn the hard way, the expensive and ego-deflating way, that they do not possess required qualifications. Often, it is not because they lack credentials but because relevant others do not accept those credentials. This is illustrated in almost every issue of the *NASW News,* which describes how social workers are challenged about their qualifications for private practice.[2] In one story, a social worker in Ohio had a successful private practice, served clients effectively, and was credited with providing a valued community service. One day, however, the state authorities said he had to suspend operations immediately. They claimed he was violating the state's psychological-licensing laws. He was practicing a "psychological service" without a license as a psychologist.[3] In another story, a social worker in a New Jersey private practice was told by the state that he was unqualified to practice marital and family therapy, because he was a social worker.[4]

These incidents illustrate the important question that must be faced by every social worker who contemplates private practice: what qualifications and credentials are necessary before one can have credibility as a private practitioner? This question raises others as well: What is the necessary training and experience? Is a license needed, and, if so, how can one be obtained? What tests have to be taken, and what preparations for them are advisable? Once in private practice, how does one prove that qualifications are up to date? Are continuing education credits required, and, if so, where are records about them kept? What is necessary for insurance companies to help pay for the services? Where is it permissible to practice and where is it not? Are private practitioners required to join any organizations? Should any be joined for acceptance and protection in the practice? To answer such questions properly, the practitioner starts by considering what it is that constitutes a qualification or credential.

Nature of Professional Qualifications

Professional qualifications are a social institution's implicit or explicit standards to which an individual or group must conform in order to have the endorsement of that institution. If, for example, the institution is a profession or a professional association, endorsement will be given only to those individuals who complete its educational and experiential requirements and meet its assurances of quality. If the institution is the legal system of the relevant jurisdiction, approval comes by obeying the laws. The institution usually, but not always, explicates its criteria for those who seek its endorsement. The endorsement is then granted to those who offer proof that they have conformed to the criteria. The proof may be offered in the form of certifying exams that must be passed, academic degrees, types of experiences, documented professional activities, or demonstrable skills.

What is offered as proof is supposedly but not necessarily relevant to the activity that is to be endorsed. What counts is whether or not the endorsing institution considers the proof to be relevant. For example, in some states, pharmacists are still required to demonstrate that they can competently mix medical compounds in order to get their licenses. In recent years, however, the nation has established such rigorous food and drug laws that virtually all prescriptions have to be made under highly controlled laboratory conditions. In effect, the ability to mix compounds in a pharmacy is irrelevant even though the pharmacist will not be endorsed without proving ability to do it. In another example, a professional social work association will not endorse an individual who does not hold a certain academic degree. The degree itself does not prove that the individual is competent to practice social work; but it does show that the person has followed a course of training that has provided information pertinent to the practice of the profession.

Although it is the institution's right to determine who it will endorse, it is the individual's right to determine the endorsements to seek. There are many individuals, groups, and institutions whose endorsement might be acquired, each with its own criteria and means of enforcement. The standards of one may be different from those of another, and the standards of the same institution may change from one time or location to the next.

The practitioner's final choice rests basically on an estimate of how much good the endorsement will do compared to how much resource expenditure it will take to meet the standards of the endorsing body. In effect, the practitioner makes a cost-benefit analysis.

Minimum Standards

The social worker who plans to enter private practice should conform at least to the standards indicated below. These elements will receive further discussion after they are summarized here.

1. Licensing. In those states that license social work practice, the worker must conform to their requirements. These usually include specified educational degrees, practice experience, state competency exams, and, occasionally, fulfilling certain continuing education requirements. There is still much variation in these requirements from state to state and from time to time, but the social worker can find out the requirements for his or her state by calling or writing to the State Board of Health Examiners or equivalent department. In a state that does not license social workers, it is important for the social worker to obtain professional certification or endorsement as discussed earlier. This then becomes the principal means of assuring a litigious public and a watchful third-party-financing system that the practice conforms to some professional standard.

2. Local Business and Zoning Laws. Because private practice is a business as well as a profession, the practitioner must usually conform to local laws pertaining to the operation of a business. In many jurisdictions, the practitioner must obtain a license to operate the business or practice. This often consists of nothing more than filing an application and paying a modest fee. The practitioner must also make sure the location of the practice does not violate zoning ordinances. This is especially crucial for home offices and any settings outside traditional office buildings. The worker can determine these requirements in advance by contacting county or city licensing and zoning offices. The names of the offices vary by jurisdiction but they are easily located in the county directory.

3. *Professional Certification.* To have credibility as a professional, the social worker also needs the endorsement of the profession. The National Association of Social Workers (NASW), the predominant social work association, endorses private practitioners primarily through certification in the Academy of Certified Social Workers (ACSW). The requirements for certification in ACSW are membership in NASW, a master's or doctoral degree from a graduate school accredited by the Council on Social Work Education, two years of fulltime practice experience after receiving the degree (or 3,000 hours of paid, part-time work), three acceptable professional references, including one from the applicant's supervisor, and a passing mark in the ACSW examination.[5] The local chapter office or the national headquarters of NASW can provide further information about how the applications can be obtained and when and where exams can be taken.

4. *Continuing Education Requirements.* To assure that the worker has kept current, some states have established continuing education requirements, but these vary from state to state and must be checked on an individual basis. Although NASW does not require continuing education of its members, it has set standards that are recommended for professional practitioners: ninety hours of continuing professional education every three years, of which forty hours must be formally organized learning events in classrooms, practice-oriented seminars, or accredited training activities and another thirty hours spent in professional meetings or symposia sponsored by social work or allied organizations. The last twenty hours may be spent in individual professional activities, such as research, teaching, writing, and independent study.[6]

    5. *Insurance Requirements for Reimbursement.* Each of the third-
party organizations that help pay the client's bill has its own requirements for reimbursement. Some will not reimburse social workers
at all, while others will pay if the social work provider meets the
standards of the profession. At present, no company knowingly reimburses for professional services if the practitioner is not licensed in
those states where licensing exists. They also do not knowingly
reimburse professionals who lack professional certification or who
belong to professional organizations that have no peer review
mechanism or quality assurance program. An increasing number of
third-party organizations now reimburse only those clients whose
treatment comes under the direct supervision of a physician. In such
cases, the social worker must meet with the physician periodically
and allow the doctor to interview the client regularly. A social worker
should ascertain the specific reimbursement requirements of a new
client's coverage before getting very far into the treatment. Clients
often expect their health insurance to cover the services of the social
worker as it does other health professionals. A financial problem for
both worker and client could occur unless this information is known
in advance. The worker can simply call the nearest office of the relevant company for their criteria for provider reimbursement. It is wise
to get this information in writing, however, to protect against future
problems.
    6. *Consumer Requirements.* In previous years, clients had to take
an approach of caveat emptor with professionals. They had few pro-
tections against incompetent or unscrupulous practitioners. However,
in recent years, consumer protection laws have rightly been applied
to professionals as well as to merchants. Consumer protection laws
and government agencies now play the role of watchdog with professionals. Professions are increasingly required to have quality
assurance programs to control their members against practices that
may be harmful to the consumer. Quality assurance programs are
imposed from outside the professions by government organizations
and from within the profession through internal peer review
mechanisms.[7] Consumers have the right to take any grievances to the
professional's peers and to sue for any damages because of wrongdoing. Thus, conscientious professionals are obliged to practice under
the auspices of organizations that have adequate quality assurance

programs, peer review provisions, and explicit standards of conduct for their members. The private practitioner who maintains NASW membership meets these requirements. NASW has a long history of strong quality assurance and peer review provisions and professional standards of conduct regulated through its Code of Ethics. The practitioner can comply further with this standard by making copies of the NASW Code of Ethics available to clients or, at least, posting one in the waiting room of the office.

7. *Personal Requirements.* The individual must also possess certain personal attributes if the practice is to succeed.[8] These characteristics are just as important as licensing, professional certification, or any other requirement is. Without these personal qualifications, the practitioner would have few clients, no referrals, financial problems, and disorganized records. First, the practitioner must have a high degree of motivation. To face and overcome all the obstacles one is likely to encounter requires that the worker be determined to be a private practitioner. If the worker is in private practice because an agency job is not available, he or she is not likely to devote the resources to making the practice viable. Furthermore, a considerable amount of energy, drive, and assertiveness are required in order to do the work. Many people do better when they are encouraged or pushed to get their work done. If motivation by others is needed, the worker is not likely to do well in private practice; it is too easy to put things off. Instead, the worker must be a self-starter who can maintain a self-imposed schedule. Also needed is a certain amount of business sense and management skills. For example, the worker has to be able to ask clients for money and to apply pressure to those who do not pay their bills. The practitioner must have financial resources to start the practice. Social workers have to spend substantial sums even before they start seeing clients and drawing revenue. They have to have enough financial support or a job to supplement the private practice income during the start-up phase. The most important personal qualities are competence and knowledge.

Practice without Minimum Qualifications

Private practitioners have been known to operate private practices without achieving even the minimum standards given above. Some people do not have appropriate licenses, certificates, education, or experience and seem to hope that no one will notice. Trying to operate a practice with less than minimum requirements is tempting to some because it seems so easy. Enforcement is still lax, and punishments are usually not severe. In those states where there is no social work licensing, the legal authorities will do nothing about private practitioners without proper credentials who call themselves social workers. Indeed, it is not uncommon for members of some specialties to call themselves social workers even though they were educated in different fields. Often, they belong to various counseling specialties that have little public or institutional recognition. Sometimes social agencies or institutions hire such people and eventually call them social workers because that is the available job title. When these people enter private practice, they retain the title, claiming they are experienced "social workers." In the absence of licensing, there can be little protection against this practice. Even the professional association can do little, except for negative publicity for the practitioner. NASW would have a strong case only if the unqualified practitioners tried to use the designation *ACSW* after their names.

Practitioners who count on inadequate laws, little enforcement, or minimal requirements to maintain their offices are shortsighted. The national trend is rapidly moving toward stronger regulations, higher standards, and more stringent means of enforcing them. There is now tremendous competition by the various professional groups to show the public and those who pay for service that high standards exist. Consumer groups and third-party organizations will require high standards even if state laws do not. Consumers will not go to practitioners who do not demonstrate competence or to agencies that lack quality assurance programs.

Anyone who hopes to remain in private practice will find it in his or her long-term interest to upgrade skills and qualifications regularly. When professions and state licensing boards impose higher standards, it may seem threatening and needlessly intrusive, but it is in the social worker's interest as well as the client's. In the near future, the only way a profession will be able to compete with other professions is through possessing and enforcing high standards. The existence of these standards will be one of the private practitioner's

greatest allies for maintaining a viable private practice. The qualifications of the social worker and the profession require taking quality assurance measures seriously and living up to them consistently.

Quality Assurance

"Quality assurance" refers to the procedures used by professional organizations to demonstrate that their services are worthy and not harmful to the consumer. In this general sense, quality assurance includes the profession's ethical code, licensing and certification requirements, competency and currency testing, peer review procedures, and any other devices used to encourage and force practitioners to live up to specified standards. Now, the term also refers to a variety of formal programs that are externally imposed on some professions by law or third-party organizations.[9] These programs essentially review the work of the professional to see that the service provided is worth the money spent on it. One typical program, the Professional Standards Review Organizations (PSROs) are federally funded committees of professional overseers in every region in the nation.[10] Originally, they controlled inpatient medical care costs and were expected to scrutinize outpatient mental health care providers as well. In recent years, federal funding for PSROs has declined, but many state organizations are filling the void by acting as overseers of professional practice.

Social work was once at the forefront of the helping professions in its quality assurance procedures, providing protection against incompetence or malevolence by its members. Long before many other professions displayed concern about protecting consumers from their own incompetent or unscrupulous members, social work had comparatively rigorous measures—a strong Code of Ethics and institutionalized use of supervision to maintain standards.[11] After receiving their MSW degrees, workers were generally employed by social agencies where their practice was supervised for several years by experienced professionals. After the supervised apprenticeship was completed, the worker was still in close association with peers in a consultative relationship. If the worker displayed deficiencies in knowledge or performance, the supervisor or agency provided extra guidance or applied pressure to upgrade skills. Often agencies encouraged and paid their employees to take courses and attend professional meetings.

Of course, not all social workers were happy with this procedure. Some studies indicated that workers saw supervisors not only as teachers and role models to socialize the newer person into the established way of doing things but also as agents controlled by the agencies.[12] They said supervision taught them to conform rather than to innovate. Other studies suggested that tensions existed between supervisors and practitioners and that workers perceived supervision as encroachment on professional judgment, responsibility, and competence.[13] Supervision may have existed more to exert the agency's bureaucratic control on its employees than to protect the consumer from incompetence, but the effect was the same—the client had some protection.

In the private practice model of delivering social services, supervision cannot be used to show the public that practitioners measure up to standard. The appropriate alternatives are the same quality assurance devices that other professions use: rigorous competency testing, enforced demonstration of practice skill, proof of currency, strong and consistent licensing and certification requirements, and formal grievance and peer review procedures. If these programs exist within the profession, they are less likely to be externally imposed.

Unfortunately, for private social work practitioners, the profession is in serious conflict about its quality assurance devices. The problems partly stem from the ambivalence of social workers themselves about standards. While many social workers continue to struggle for licensing and other regulation, many of their colleagues resist such ideas. They fear, perhaps with justification, that they will become victims of discrimination or that they will not be able or willing to conform to the standards. Many social workers want to raise educational standards for entry into the profession, while many others advocate a greater role for the BSW social worker, even in private practice. Many competent social workers resist the idea of competency testing because they fear that it would be too clinically oriented. They advocate that the profession should assume more of a macro than micro perspective and think such measures take the profession in the wrong direction. NASW cannot force its members to accept higher or different standards; it is not a monolithic autocracy

that makes and hands down decisions for its members to accept, whether or not they agree. NASW reflects the mood of its members, and, if the members are in conflict with one another, the professional association can only mirror the internal turmoil that results. The profession and its private practice sector will have difficulty gaining public acceptance without unity.

Licensing Issues

In 1969, the NASW Delegate Assembly, the governing body of the association, resolved that social work would henceforth pursue licensing of practice within each state.[14] The profession adopted the resolution in the belief that it was in the public interest that individuals who provide social work services be sufficiently trained and be held to publicly described requirements of qualifications and performance. The objective was to get every state to license the practice of social work, and not just the title.

To achieve this objective, NASW proposed a Model Licensing Act for the legislatures of every state. The proposed licensing regulation contained several provisions: The license would (1) apply to all levels of practice, (2) include criteria for autonomous and private practice, (3) include valid means of testing social workers for competence, (4) cover all social work specialties and settings, (5) contain continuing education requirements, and (6) require professional accountability.

In the years since the resolution was passed, several states have established licensing statutes containing some of the requirements, but there is still no state in the nation in which all the provisions have been included. The major barrier is that the profession has had a difficult time defining what competent social work practice is and specifying how licensed practice differs from unlicensed.

Hardcastle analyzed the issue and offered some disturbing conclusions.[15] After finding many shortcomings in the licensing qualifications of every state, he said that the current method of licensing has little potential for the protection of the public or for the development of the profession. This is so, he asserts, because the statutes lack precise definitions about what knowledge and skills are needed to distinguish competence from incompetence. If competence cannot be defined and tested, how can licensing be useful in specifying who is or is not qualified to practice? If practice can be precisely defined but is not tested and monitored, one wonders about the basic ethics of the profession. The regulations are worthless unless they distinguish between those who are and those who are not capable of social work practice. Actually, weak regulations are virtually useless; if they are on the books and yet have no real regulating or distinguishing power, their existence makes it more difficult to legislate stronger regulations.

The private practitioner should be more concerned than any other segment of the profession about the existence of strong and enforceable public licensing. Because the private practitioner is essentially unsupervised and outside agency control, public and professional recognition of competence is the principal way to achieve public credibility and public funding for practice.

Competency-Testing Issues

The licensing bottleneck stems largely from inadequate means of distinguishing competent from incompetent practice. Progress will remain impeded until better measures are found to make such distinctions. Yet, the profession has not been overly zealous in its efforts to test its members for competency. There is an assumption that the way to determine professional competence is primarily through education; those who acquire the right degrees are deemed competent. Obviously, professional education is necessary, although not sufficient, for making such a distinction. Education alone does not assure the consumer that the worker knows what to do.

Most of the other helping professions, including psychology, nursing, and psychiatry, have made progress with their competency-testing efforts. Their professional associations frequently sponsor exams that must be passed in order to retain membership. In most cases, members have to pass additional tests periodically to demonstrate that they have kept current. In most states, a license to practice is contingent on passing state-regulated tests.

Social workers, however, have little opportunity to demonstrate their proficiency through exams. They only have two possible tests— the ACSW certification exam and the licensing exams for some states—and the vast majority of social workers are not required to take them. The ACSW exam has been required for certification only since 1971, and state-licensing exams are required in only 15 states.

In those states where competency exams are required for social work licensing, there has been considerable controversy and dissatisfaction. For example, in his study of the California licensing exam, Borenzweig found many problems.[16] About one-fourth of the applicants failed, but those who passed thought the test was too general and didn't adequately test their knowledge. Most of the applicants said the administration of the exam was deficient, that it permitted cheating, and that it was not conducted in an atmosphere conducive to test taking. There was no correlation between passing the exam and age, experience, fieldwork, training, credentials of supervisors, or type of concentrations in education programs. Only one variable seemed to matter. Social workers who had received personal psychotherapy before taking the test were more likley to pass than those who had not. California has taken steps to improve this situation since the Borenzweig study, but such cannot be said for the majority of other states in which social workers are engaged in private practice.

The ACSW exam is administered twice yearly in a number of test centers nationwide.[17] It consists of 175 multiple choice questions developed with the help of the Princeton Educational Testing Service and it is administered under NASW auspices. The exam is given not just to clinical specialists but to all those who seek the title "Certified Social Worker." The test attempts to be comprehensive, covering the range of knowledge and skill that is supposed to be within the social worker's grasp. The exam is a test of generic social work knowledge with a heavy emphasis on social work values, principles, and methods from community to individual interventions.

Passing the exam and becoming certified does not assure the practitioner of great approbation. The public still seems to have little awareness of its meaning, and third-party organizations and overseeing bodies still do not see it as a way of assuring conformity to high standards. Although the profession and most private practitioners encourage ACSW certification, one need not be an ACSW to be a qualified private practitioner in almost every state. However, the ACSW title is a step in the right direction. As the public and other professions become more aware of the relevance of the title, it will grow in importance.

Requirements for Keeping Current

The knowledge base for social workers in private practice keeps growing. A practitioner who does not keep up with the advances in the field is not conforming to professional social work standards. Of course, the same is true for the other professions in private and agency practice; every five years medical doctors have to acquire half again as much knowledge as they obtained in medical school just to keep up with advances in their profession[18]; psychologists have a knowledge half-life of ten to twelve years.[19] Professionals who do not maintain knowledge of the field do a disservice to themselves and their clients; some call it negligence.

What can the profession do to assure the public and the overseers that the practitioner has kept up? What can be done to encourage or force unmotivated practitioners to stay abreast of new knowledge? Most professions rely on two possibilities: recertification of members through periodic testing and enforced continuing education requirements.[20] Social work is behind most of the other professions in pursuing both possibilities.

Continuing education standards for social workers are rarely imposed or enforced. State licensing laws have different requirements for continuing education. Of the states that licensed social workers in 1983, only ten had mandatory continuing education requirements.[21] Only one of these—Colorado—specified the number of continuing education units required. The other nine states leave the amount to be specified by the state licensing board. Other licensing states typically renew social work licenses simply when the renewal fee is paid; in some states, even this is not necessary.

NASW's requirement of ninety hours of continuing education every three years is not rigorously enforced. The association does not keep records of how many units each member has acquired, as do some professional associations. It does not monitor the quality of the educational experience that the member receives. The member is on the honor system when it comes to keeping track of relevant units.

Some social workers justify the lack of enforced continuing education. They correctly point out that the continuing education movement is on the wane in all professions, including social work. There has been a lack of evidence to show a relationship between continuing education and continuing competence.[22] If a person is no more competent with continuing education than without it, what is the purpose of requiring it? Obviously, the same argument could be applied to requiring attendance at schools of social work in the absence of adequate competency testing, but that is another issue. In any event, testing, not training, is seen as the more appropriate way of proving that the person has kept current.

There is little in the way of periodic examinations and recertification requirements to determine if social workers have updated their knowledge. Nurses, lawyers, physicians, and psychologists take tests every few years to assure the public they are maintaining skills and knowledge.[23] Psychiatrists must be recertified every six years by passing a multiple choice exam of 400 items and an oral test. They are eligible to take the exam after they have taken a specified number of continuing education units.[24] Some might argue that the exam and the education do not prove psychiatric competence, but, at the very least, it has some public relations value. The requirement tells the public, third-party underwriters, and government overseers that efforts to encourage currency standards are in effect. Social workers have little that is comparable. They have not pushed to institute recertification exams either at the state or professional level; thus, there are few ways that a private practitioner can prove up-to-date knowledge.

Many social workers not only resist currency examinations but defend a norm, the grandfather clause, that undercuts and precludes them. Grandfathering is the practice of automatically granting an experienced social worker the same credentials, licenses, and professional certifications granted to younger workers merely because they obtained the necessary qualifications prior to a certain date. It assumes (1) that social work knowledge and skill, once acquired, are mastered for life, or (2) that the profession is not generating new knowledge and skills. Only if knowledge and skill are static would there be any reason to assume the worker would not need to show up-to-date knowledge. Nevertheless, social workers who received their ACSW certificates before an exam was instituted in 1971 have not been required to take the exam to retain their certificates.[25] In most states, social workers who received the ACSW certificate before 1971 simply have to pay renewal fees in order to renew their licenses and to hold current ACSW membership.

Peer Review Requirements

It is very important for private practitioners to have a mechanism by which their professional colleagues can evaluate their practice. Peer review is now mandated by government and third-party-financing organizations as a way of assuring the public that a profession and any one of its members measures up to the standard. Third parties are increasingly reluctant to pay practitioners whose profession does not have such a system. Peer review is also important for private practice; it can provide a balance for the lack of supervision or peer consultation that generally occurs in agencies. Peer review mechanisms are also demanded by consumers and consumer groups. Clients are entitled to the opportunity to express any grievances or alleged wrongdoing by the professional to the practitioner's peers. Private practitioners benefit by the procedure by preserving their credibility. The reputation of the profession itself could be harmed if a member continued working at lower than professional standards with no accountability.

All traditional helping professions have peer review systems but each has different objectives and procedures for implementing them. Some use the system only to adjudicate grievances lodged with the profession by unhappy clients. Others use peer review as a way to encourage members to improve certain practices even though no complaint has been made. Some procedures are very informal, consisting merely of regular meetings of professionals who teach each other; others are formal, with prescribed procedures, elected officers, and appeal procedures. Social work already compares favorably with the other professions in its peer review procedures and is now at work to upgrade them even further.[26] NASW's system is primarily concerned with adjudicating grievances brought against members. Each NASW chapter maintains a standing or an ad hoc committee on inquiry comprising designated chapter members. When a complaint is filed, the committee has to act rapidly. Within ten days the

chapter must inform the complainant that action is being taken. Hearings begin within forty-five days if the complaint meets the necessary criteria, and a written report with recommendations must appear in another forty-five days. If there is no appeal, the recommendations are implemented within four months. When the committee rules against a member, membership in NASW may be temporarily suspended, or the member may be given a written reprimand and have his or her practice monitored for a specified time. Private practitioners could be required to receive approved supervision, and the fees they receive from the client could be waived for a specified time.

Considering that NASW has over 90,000 members, remarkably few complaints have ever been adjudicated. During the first 22 years that the procedure was in effect nationwide, only 154 cases were processed. The rate has been increasing in recent years, however. Most of the cases result from disputes between NASW members and agency managers; only 13 percent come from client complaints.

Studies about the procedure have shown that there is still a need for members of the profession and social work consumers to become more familiar with social work methods and practice and with the reasonable expectations to be derived from social work intervention.[27] The revised NASW Code of Ethics is clearer, more comprehensive, and more definitive than its predecessor, and it is expected that this will make it easier for social workers and their consumers to understand the standards better.

Credentials for Reimbursement through Insurance

Third-party financial organizations, such as insurance companies and government organizations, have increased influence on the way mental health care is provided. Although they have no legal authority to say what are appropriate social work credentials, they have the right to say what credentials will be required if they are going to reimburse the provider. So far, the insurance companies and government financing bodies have not been uniform about their criteria for reimbursement. Moreover, the criteria have been changing rapidly for all mental health care providers, including social workers.

Blue Cross/Blue Shield, the largest health insurer, only began to pay for mental health care in the middle 1960s. In the 1970s, it greatly expanded its coverage, made payments more generous for mental health care, and made more professions eligible for reimbursement. Now, however, this trend is reversing. Coverage and provider eligibility has come to be more restricted. Psychiatrists are now the only professionals who do not need supervision for reimbursement in any state. Psychologists are directly reimbursable without psychiatric supervision in about half the states. Many other professions and disciplines are not eligible for Blue Cross reimbursement, even if supervision does take place.

Social work remains eligible in most Blue Cross localities, but only when certain criteria are met. The social worker has to be state licensed where applicable. The insured client has to have a medical (DSM-III) diagnosis, and a physician has to make a specific referral to the social worker for treatment. Many social workers have difficulty meeting the requirement that treatment has to take place under a physician's supervision. An additional Blue Cross requirement is that the physician has to discuss the case with the social worker at least once a month and has to interview the client at least once annually. The physician has to document this to Blue Cross whenever reimbursement forms are submitted. The physician who "supervises" the social worker for this purpose does not have to be a psychiatrist or know much mental health care.

Other insurance companies have somewhat different eligibility requirements. For example, the coverage by Aetna Life and Casualty Company, which is one of the largest insurers for health care in the nation, is more restrictive for social workers. Like Blue Cross, it also reimburses social work under the supervision of a physician, but it does not specify that the supervision must take place every month or that the client must be seen periodically after the referral is made. However, Aetna places a much lower reimbursement limit on the number of visits a client may make to a therapist.

One insurance program with very important implications for social work is the government system for military families. The Civilian Hospital and Medical Providers for the Uniformed Services (CHAMPUS) reimburses military families who need health care when there are no military hospital providers available. All dependents of military personnel (not the military person himself) and all retired military careerists can be reimbursed for civilian health care as part of their benefits packages. The beneficiary is reimbursed for 80 percent of the provider's reasonable bill or 75 percent of the bill if the sponsor is retired. The beneficiary pays the first fifty dollars of the provider's bill each fiscal year.

CHAMPUS is the closest thing the nation has to a government-regulated and -funded medical care program. The regulations and provisions that CHAMPUS adopts are carefully noted by the private insurance companies and often used as models for their own programs. It is thought by many that if national health insurance is established, this may well be its prototype.

The Department of Defense specifies which professions are eligible as health care providers and what the requirements are for their continued eligibility. When the program was first instituted in 1968, social work was eligible for autonomous reimbursement. The only requirement was that a military physician had to diagnose a client and refer him to the social worker. Since then, the Department of Defense has challenged social work's inclusion as an independent provider on several occasions. Like Blue Cross and Aetna, it now requires social workers to provide their services under medical supervision.

Most social workers in private practice are insulted by the requirement that their work occur under medical supervision. It is, they say, an abrogation of their right to be considered autonomous professionals and demeans social work by putting it in the position of being an extension of or subordinate to another profession. The insurance companies have a ready response: The point out that they are health insurers, that they reimburse for treatment of health problems, including mental health disorders, but that they are not insuring against social injustice or social dysfunctions. Only where social work is concerned with providing health services are they involved, therefore coverage must be under the auspices of a health professional. Their reluctance to reimburse also stems from the fact that competence is difficult to judge since exams and currency standards are in transition, many states do not have licensing, and little enforcement of standards occurs in the licensed states.

This is not to imply that insurance companies are the enemy of social workers. Even medicine and psychiatry are having considerable trouble these days. Furthermore, it is in the economic interests of insurance companies to consider social workers as appropriate and reimbursable providers. If different disciplines are competing, the costs should be less than if a single profession monopolizes service delivery. CHAMPUS recently completed a study showing that social work costs are significantly less than those of other disciplines for the same service.[28] However, whether or not third parties endorse social work as a valid provider will depend on the willingness of the profession to enhance its standards and qualifications for practice.

Notes and References

1. County Board of Appeals for Montgomery County, Md., Case No. A-197. (Mimeographed.)

2. National Association of Social Workers, "Association Assists Members in Litigation On Right To Practice," *NASW News,* 26 (November 1981), p. 10.

3. Ibid., p. 10.

4. Ibid., p. 10.

5. Ruth R. Middleman, *A Study Guide for ACSW Certification* (Washington, D.C.: National Association of Social Workers, 1981), p. 9.

6. "Standards for Continuing Professional Education," NASW Policy Statement No. 10 (Silver Spring, Md.: National Association of Social Workers, 1982).

7. Claudia J. Coulton, *Social Work Quality Assurance Programs: A Comparative Analysis* (Washington, D.C.: National Association of Social Workers, 1979), p. 7; and Coulton, "Quality Assurance for Social Service Programs: Lessons from Health Care," *Social Work,* 27 (September 1982), pp. 397–402.

8. Robert Barker, *The Business of Psychotherapy: Private Practice Administration for Therapists, Counselors, and Social Workers* (New York: Columbia University Press, 1982), pp. 72–74.

9. Claudia C. Lorish, "Examining Quality Assurance Systems," *Health and Social Work,* 2 (May 1977), pp. 20–41.

10. U.S. Department of Health, Education and Welfare, *PSRO Program Manual* (Washington, D.C.: U.S. Government Printing Office, 1978), pp. 730–732.

11. Charles S. Levy, "The Ethics of Supervision," *Social Work,* 18 (March 1973), pp. 114–121.

12. See, for example, Herbert Aptekar, "Supervision and the Development of Professional Responsibility: An Application of Systems Thought," *Jewish Social Work Forum,* 3 (Fall 1965), pp. 4–17.

13. See, for example, Nina Toren, "Semi-Professionalism and Social Work," in Amitai Etzioni, ed., *The Semi-Professions and Their Organizations* (New York: Free Press, 1969), pp. 153–157.

14. National Association of Social Workers, "New Policy Statement On Licensing Issued," *NASW News,* 19 (September 1974), p. 12.

15. David A. Hardcastle, "Public Regulation of Social Work," *Social Work,* 22 (January 1977), pp. 14–20.

16. Herman Borenzweig, "Who Passes the California Licensing Examinations?" *Social Work,* 22 (May 1977), pp. 173–177.

17. Middleman, *A Study Guide for ACSW Certification,* p. 9.

18. Carolyn Robinowitz and Milton Greenblatt, "Continuing Certification and Continuing Education," *American Journal of Psychiatry,* 137 (March 1980), pp. 292–299.

19. S. S. Dubin, "Obsolescence or Lifelong Education: A Choice for the Professional," *American Psychologist,* 36 (June 1981), pp. 486–498.

20. Cyril Houle, *Continuing Learning in the Professions* (San Francisco: Jossey-Bass, 1980), pp. 280–286.

21. Richard L. Edwards and Ronald K. Green, "Mandatory Continuing Education: Time for Reevaluation," *Social Work,* 28 (January–February 1983), pp. 43–48.

22. Ibid., p. 46.

23. U.S. Department of Health, Education and Welfare, *Credentialing Health Manpower* (Washington, D.C.: U.S. Government Printing Office, 1978), pp. 16–17.

24. Steven Sharfstein, "Private Psychiatry and Accountability," *American Journal of Psychiatry,* 135 (November 1978), pp. 43–47.

25. Lois G. Swack, "Continuing Education and Changing Needs," *Social work,* 20 (November 1975), pp. 474–480.

26. *Procedures for the Adjudication of Grievances* (Washington, D.C.: National Association of Social Workers, 1970, revised 1978).

27. David J. Warfel, Dennis M. Maloney, and Karen Blase, "Consumer Feedback in Human Service Programs," *Social Work,* 26 (March 1981), pp. 151–156.

28. National Association of Social Workers, "CHAMPUS Experiment: Survey Supports Vendorship," *NASW News,* 27 (October 1982), p. 8.

5

ESTABLISHING A VIABLE PRACTICE

O nce the social worker feels qualified for private practice and is willing to take the necessary risks, attention can be shifted to the pleasant task of getting a practice established. This means advanced planning; otherwise, the social worker is likely to encounter many avoidable problems.

Before opening an office and certainly before seeing the first fee-for-service private clients, the practitioner has many important decisions to make, including the kind of practice to develop and the kind of clientele to attract. The practitioner must consider where to locate and how to equip an office and how to finance the business in its developing stages. The practitioner should know the jurisdiction's legal regulations for small businesses and professional practices and must look into malpractice and business liability insurance. Plans for retirement and for insurance against illness or incapacitation need to be established. The practitioner must determine how to satisfy the income, property, and professional tax requirements of the tax collectors, including federal and local authorities. If helpers are employed, either part or full time, the employer must consider how to fulfill the legal requirements for their social security, retirement, and employment compensation program. It is important to establish a consistent policy for client fees from the beginning. Money issues to resolve include how much to charge, how to get clients to pay their bills on time, how to get insurance companies to pay for services, and whether or not to have a fixed or sliding fee scale. Once these decisions are made and the implementation worked out, the practitioner will feel more comfortable about devoting attention to the tasks of effectively providing quality service for clients.

Financial Management System

The first practical step in establishing a private practice is to develop a system for keeping track of finances. This system should be put into effect before the first client is seen—even before any efforts are made to get referrals. A financial system is as important for agency-employed social workers who want to see only a few clients privately as it is for those contemplating full-time private practice. Fortunately, it takes little time, effort, or money to develop a good system and it will prove to be of inestimable value once the practice is established. The system should include a business checking account, a financial ledger, a separate tax record, a procedure for keeping track of payments due and payments made by each client, and a procedure for handling and tracking all financial transactions.

Business Checking Account

A checking account solely for practice expenditures and receipts should be established first. It is highly desirable to have a complete record of all receipts and expenditures going through one account; this provides a valuable cross-reference for the practitioner's financial record and is also very useful to tax auditors and accountants. Although it is tempting to wait until the address of the practice office is determined so that it can be placed on the check, the establishment of an account should not be delayed for this reason. Money will be spent to establish the practice before clients are seen and fees collected, and these early expenses should be handled through the permanent business account.

In the beginning, money is "loaned" to the business account from personal funds or from a bank loan; later it is expected that revenues will be sufficient to cover overhead, provide an income for the practitioner, and repay the initial "loan."

The business checking account must be kept separate from the worker's personal checking account. The only checks written on it will be those directly related to running the practice; the only money placed in the account, apart from the clearly designated initial loan, is from clients' payments. Ultimately, the amount left in the account after all practice expenses have been met is the practitioner's "salary," and a check should periodically be drawn on these funds (if any) for the practitioner.

Finance Ledger

The first check written should be to buy a financial ledger. This can be as simple as a tablet of columnar accounting sheets or as elaborate as a personally designed accounting system developed by a management consultant. Many private practitioners use a standard loose-leaf notebook in which are kept, in one place, all pertinent financial records for the practice. The first page in this book can be a columnar ledger sheet used only to record income. Whenever a payment is made, by check or in cash, by or in behalf of the client, an entry is made in ink on this sheet. The entry includes the date the money was received, the name of the client, and the amount of payment. Every line on this page is eventually filled, leaving no space blank. This assures tax auditors that receipts are not being omitted. Periodically, when these funds are deposited in the business checking account, the totals are added on the sheet. The total on the ledger should be the same as the amount deposited (this is even more reassuring to the Internal Revenue Service [IRS]). Clients should be given or sent receipts for payment so that they also have a record of payment.

The next sheet in the finance book is for disbursements. Again, each line is filled in ink, with an indication of when a bill was paid, who was paid, and the amount. If possible, every expenditure for the practice should be paid by check from the office account so that the checking account and the disbursements page are the same. This also includes all checks written for the social worker's "salary." For tax purposes, an item is considered paid when a valid check for it is written, rather than when the bill comes in.

As these sheets become filled, they are totaled, removed from the notebook, and placed in a file folder. In this folder also goes all other financial information that pertains to the practice for the tax year. The receipts and disbursements sheets are of such importance that the worker may want to make copies and keep the extras in a different safe place. At tax time, the practitioner should have a clear record of all financial activity.

The loose-leaf notebook also contains, in alphabetical order, a separate sheet for each client detailing their financial transactions with the practitioner. At the top of each sheet is space to put pertinent information about the client: insurance company number, social security number, name, address, place of work, and telephone numbers. The sheet is lined and columned and can indicate such things about the client as date seen, type of service provided (group therapy, individual therapy, family therapy, colateral visit, environmental work), and charge for service. Some practitioners also indicate on these sheets how much the client owes, how much the insurance company paid, and when payments were made. These sheets are updated by making an entry on them with every client meeting or financial transaction. They can be copied, and the copy can constitute a bill, which is sent to the client. When the client's case is closed and outstanding amounts paid, these sheets may be removed from the notebook and included in the client's case record file. This method makes it possible to keep client financial information separate from the case record, which should be done, lawyers say, to minimize malpractice complications and other legal problems.

This system entails a double entry in the receipts sheet and on the client's finance sheet, which is also helpful in reducing the chances of mistakes. Some practitioners who use this system also have a third entry in the form of notations in their appointment books. They keep this book with them at all times and record in it, beside each client's name and the date seen, when a payment was made. They also note when a practice expense was paid on the appropriate date. All this may seem overly cautious, but it is actually very simple, takes little time, and keeps the accounts in order.[1]

Social workers thinking about entering private practice should read one or more of the many available guides to accounting for small businesses in order to become familiar with basic principles.[2] One of the most useful of these guides is the IRS's *Tax Guide for Small Businesses.*[3]

Malpractice and Office Liability Insurance

The second step in establishing a practice is to become insured against the risks of malpractice and office liabilities. After reading about the malpractice risks in chapter 3, it should be obvious why there should be no client contact—actual or potential—until this coverage is obtained. Many commercial insurance companies underwrite social work malpractice risks, and their premiums are low. Presently, the NASW-sponsored plan has the best rates and coverage generally available. The agency-employed social worker can easily transfer or add malpractice coverage obtained for the agency practice to a private practice setting at minimal rate changes.

The practitioner will also need office liability insurance. This coverage takes care of anyone who is accidentally injured on the practitioner's premises. Liability policies cover against risks not protected under the malpractice insurance. These policies are analogous to homeowner's insurance and may also cover against vandalism, theft, and weather damage to the office facilities. The rates are low and available from most commercial homeowner insurance companies. It is worthwhile to have even if a practitioner is in part-time private practice and using another professional's office. Coverage should certainly be obtained when the office is in the planning stages so that the practitioner will not have to wait to see clients for the few weeks it might take to get coverage.

The private practitioner, especially one no longer affiliated with an agency, may also want insurance against sickness and resulting loss of income and permanent disability. Many companies offer such coverage, but nongroup rates can be very high. The NASW-sponsored plan for health, income loss, and disability has rates and coverage that are quite competitive.[4]

Partnerships and Group Practices

The next stage in this planning process concerns other people with whom the practitioner will work—whether the practice will be an individual or group practice and whether secretarial and maintenance help, consultants, accountants, and business managers will be employed. Once these decisions are made, location and size of office space can be determined.

For most, partnerships are more desirable than individual practice. Not only are there substantial cost savings in sharing office space, but the feeling of isolation is reduced and coverage during illnesses or vacations is possible. Partners can provide more specialized services and allow the use of team models in providing social or interprofessional services. In-house consultation is readily available. Partners can be sources of companionship and morale boosters and the arrangement can help avoid burnout.[5] Of course, if the partners are not compatible because of different tastes or noncomplimentary types of clients, there can be problems. Problems can also occur over sharing equipment and keeping track of expenditures.

In unincorporated partnerships, the practitioners usually share office expenses equally and do not share receipts. In some more formal arrangements or corporations, the organization pays all expenses and the practitioners are paid a specified percentage of the total receipts. It is better for new social work practitioners to try a less formal partnership first to see if the situation is compatible. In any case, the terms of the partnership, whether formalized or simply based on sharing some equipment and space, should be described in writing. A written contract or written descriptions of mutual obligations can alleviate many potential disputes and increase the possibility of a congenial and effective working relationship.

Partners may or may not be members of the same profession. There are advantages and disadvantages to both types of arrangements. When the social worker's partner is another social worker, their working methods are understandable to one another. They can usually cover each other's clients during absences because their intervention strategies are likely to be similar. Newcomers to social work can enter private practice sooner and get supervision with a qualified experienced social work partner. Working with members of other professions has the advantage of broadening the range of services the office provides.[6] It is also useful to have different viewpoints on hand. If the partner is a physician, there are fewer problems about medical backup and third-party involvement. Psychologists, marital therapists, and other specialists also bring unique areas of expertise to a partnership.

Many social workers who want to establish partnerships have trouble finding professionals similarly inclined. They can seek partners by perusing the growing number of advertisements in professional journals and professional association newspapers and newsletters, but it is usually unwise to make a commitment under such circumstances. A better way is to develop working relationships with fellow professionals. Ideally, this could occur, for example, through working together in a professional organization on a committee project. This establishes whether the potential partners can work together as they are becoming acquainted. If the worker wants a partner from another profession, volunteering on civic projects or working for political causes, hospitals, and institutions will lead to many potential associations. This will take much longer, but the decision about a partner is important enough to deserve this kind of patience.

Consultants and Employees

Before the office is established, it is also the time for the practitioner to think about employing a management consultant or a tax accountant. The worth of business and professional management consultants is most obvious during the planning stages. A management consultant can advise the beginning practitioner on bookkeeping procedures, tax records, tax savings, investment programs, retirement accounts, and many other aspects of the business. After the practice is well established, the worker may want to forego help from a management consultant and employ an accountant who specializes in income tax. The accountant may keep all the worker's books but is usually needed only for annual assistance with taxes. Management consultants and accountants, while rather expensive, usually pay for themselves by finding savings and ways to make the practice more efficient.

Many private social work practitioners also find it valuable to employ professional consultants. They may be colleagues who are more experienced and who assume some of the functions of the agency supervisor. The consultants may be social workers or members of other professions. Usually, they have private or agency practices of their own. Private practitioners would regularly go to their offices to discuss cases and sometimes even send their clients there for further evaluation.

Consultant Colleagues

Many practitioners hire experienced, professionally certified social workers as professional consultants to act as supervisors in order to help the practitioners meet the ACSW certification requirement for 3,000 hours of supervised work. However, a professional consultant is valuable even for the private practitioner who has had ample skill and experience. The consultant may be a professional colleague who does not claim to be more competent or expert but can look at a case and the intervention used more objectively. No matter how qualified one is, looking at one's work through the eyes of another is, on occasion, a good learning experience. It also means the worker is ultimately going to provide better and more effective service to the client. Often, in partnerships or shared office situations, consultation arrangements are made between the partners. In these cases, there is usually no charge because the partners reciprocate equally. Otherwise, the social worker pays a consultant the latter's standard fee for the amount of time.

Physician Consultation

Many social workers employ the services of a physician in addition to or instead of their professional colleague for regular professional consultations. There are several reasons for this. If the cases have medical backup, the worker can more easily rule out the physical origins of problems. Medication can be prescribed and monitored, and, when necessary, hospitalizations can be facilitated. Finally, the physician consultation facilitates reimbursement for social work services from some insurance companies. As indicated in an earlier chapter, in such cases, the social worker would send some clients to the physician for evaluative interviews; the worker would also see the physician on a regular basis to discuss the relevant cases. This practice is not encouraged by the social work profession because it is tantamount to saying that one profession is under the supervision of another, but, with increasing third-party involvement, this is becoming an expedient used by many private social work practitioners.

Secretarial Services

The private practitioner also needs to make decisions about secretarial and custodial help. This decision, unlike those above, need not be made until the office is set up. The activities of a private practitioner rarely require the services of a full-time secretary, but part-time help is very valuable. Two social workers sharing space might need one secretary approximately twenty hours weekly. The secretary could prepare monthly bills, fill out insurance forms, type letters, keep files orderly, receive clients in person or on the telephone, procure supplies, and maintain the office. Many workers economize by doing such tasks themselves, but it is an inefficient frugality. Hiring a person for a few hours weekly is not very expensive, and the social worker is freed to carry out those tasks that enhance practice skills and build clientele.

Employee Benefits

When employees are hired, the law says they are entitled to certain benefits.[7] If they work full time and the practitioner has a federally regulated retirement plan, all employees must be included in the plan to provide for their retirements. Part-time employees must also be covered for worker's benefits, such as unemployment and on-the-job injury compensation. Before employing anyone, the practitioner should contact the state department of labor for all the necessary forms and regulations. Other employee benefits are optional and should be negotiated before hiring takes place. Benefits, other than direct fees for service, are not required for consultants.

Professional Corporations

The decisions about whether or not to incorporate can also be made before the practice is established, although it is possible to start the practice and incorporate later. It has become quite common to see such designations as "John Smith, MD, PA" on professional stationery and shingles. Many believe that incorporating covers the purchase of yachts, large cars, cottages in the Caribbean, and unlimited luxuries without many tax consequences. In fact, professional corporations provide no more benefits of this type than exist without incorporating. Business corporations can write off these expenses when the company owns such luxuries to enhance its profitability, but any purchase must be justifiably needed to operate or improve the business or practice in order to write it off. The possibility to do this exists for unincorporated practitioners, too. Another misconception of incorporating is for a person to believe that a practitioner's personal assets are separate from business assets. In case of litigation, says this premise, only the practice assets are vulnerable. Again, although this may be true of other businesses, it is not so with professional corporations. Malpractice suits are still filed against the practitioner as well as against the corporation.

Incorporating offers some benefits, however, and should be considered, particularly if a group private practice is contemplated.[8] The major advantage is in insurance payments. Life and disability insurance premiums may be paid with pretax dollars by the corporation in the practitioner's behalf. The unincorporated practitioner pays these premiums after paying income taxes. Furthermore, much of the practitioner's medical and dental expenses may be deducted by a corporation, but the unincorporated practitioner can only deduct the standard 3 percent of adjusted gross income for health care costs. The 1982 tax law changes eliminated what had been the best reason to incorporate. Then the unincorporated practitioner could set aside only 15 percent or $15,000 of net income for tax-deferred retirement. Practitioners in the higher income brackets found this quite limiting. Through incorporating, they could set aside substantially more. Since 1984, the amounts that can be set aside for tax-deferred retirement have been increased up to $30,000. This negates the tax advantage of incorporating for all practitioners who net less than $100,000 annually.

Incorporation can cost the practitioner over $1,000 to establish and several hundred dollars annually to maintain. It requires formal record keeping, appointment of officers, and regular meetings of those officers. These costs are no longer offset by tax savings except for practitioners in very high income brackets. Any worker who reaches such income levels should retain a management or investment consultant and discuss any further advantages of incorporating.

Retirement Programs

Practitioners may also want to establish their retirement plans before they establish their practices. The plans, except for social security, are optional but may be opened with minimal initial investment and maintained with minimum or no regular contribution. If the accounts are established in advance, the contributions made to them can follow the fortunes of the practice and provide considerable income tax savings.

Keogh and TEFRA Plans

Prior to 1984, the foundation for the private practitioner's retirement planning was the federally regulated Keogh Plan for self-employed taxpayers. Keogh permitted the social worker, whether in part- or full-time practice, to set aside 15 percent of net practice receipts (or up to $15,000) per year and pay no income tax on this money until retirement. TEFRA (Tax Equity and Fiscal Responsibility Act) was designed to replace Keogh and provide more retirement protections for employees. TEFRA now permits the private practitioner to set aside up to 25 percent of net earnings (or up to $30,000) per year in certain defined circumstances. The TEFRA rules are more rigorous in providing eligibility and vesting requirements for the practitioner's employees, but otherwise they differ little from the Keogh Plan. In both cases, the worker does not begin to withdraw the money until age 59½ and must begin to withdraw it by age 70; if the money is withdrawn before this time, tax on it will be paid at the current income rate, plus a 10 percent penalty levied by the IRS. If the practitioner becomes permanently disabled before this time, withdrawals may be made without penalty. The money is held in a government-designated and government-regulated financial institution that is set up for TEFRA and Keogh programs. The worker may choose among a variety of investment possibilities by informing the institution where to invest these funds. Most private social work practitioners have their retirement accounts held in banks and the money is invested in a bank's own program or in mutual funds, stocks, or insurance annuity programs. It is remarkably easy to establish a retirement account of this type by contacting almost any bank, securities brokerage firm, or insurance company.

Individual Retirement Accounts

The social work practitioner can defer taxes until retirement through the popular Individual Retirement Accounts (IRAs), too. Even when withholding the maximum allowed in the Keogh or TEFRA Plan, an additional $2,000 can still be set aside in a tax-deferred account; the worker's spouse can also set aside up to the same amount. The rules for IRAs are in other respects almost identical to Keogh or TEFRA plans. The prudent practitioner might do well to establish an IRA account with a financial institution different than the TEFRA trustee. However, these organizations are so highly regulated and comparable that they are all relatively safe.[9]

When retirement comes, the worker may withdraw from either

or both the TEFRA and IRA accounts in a lump sum or in incre-
ments, or an insurance annuity may be purchased to assure that savings won't be outlived. At retirement, income tax is paid only on
the amount withdrawn.

Social Security (OASDHI)

Although the TEFRA and IRA programs may be optional, social
security—Old Age, Survivors, Disability, and Health Insurance
(OASDHI)—is not. Because private practitioners are not receiving
checks from employers who make FICA withholdings, the private
practitioner pays directly. The payment is automatically taken from
the quarterly income tax payment. When federal and local income
taxes are calculated each year, the private practitioner includes a
form for social security. Thus, no special actions need to be taken
for this until tax time.

Income and Other Taxes

Private practitioners, like all self-employed persons, are required by
the IRS to estimate their annual taxable income at the beginning
of the year or when they first open their practice. Based on this
estimate, they fill out a form each quarter and send it with a check
for one-fourth the total tax estimate to the IRS. If the practitioner
makes an estimate that turns out to be too low when the year-end
tax is figured, the additional tax and a penalty must be paid. This
need not happen, however, because the practitioner can easily raise
the estimate each quarter if earnings exceed the estimate. If taxes
are overestimated the practitioner gets the refund but no interest.

   If net income rises rapidly after entering private practice, the practitioner's taxes will greatly increase. Because the private practitioner
pays taxes directly instead of through payroll withholding, there can
be a difficult adjustment process. One way to lessen the crunch is
through "income averaging." In effect, the practitioner can, for tax
purposes, spread the increased earnings over several years when
earnings are lower. It is advisable to employ a certified public accountant to help with the first year's taxes if income averaging seems
a possibility.

   State and local income taxation, if applicable, is usually based on federal regulations and rates, but some localities tax the incomes of professional practices even if the jurisdiction has no personal income tax. Many jurisdictions have property taxes on the contents of a practitioner's office. The practitioner would do well to get this information from the local jurisdiction's tax bureau. It may be tempting to ignore this, in hope that no one will notice, but eventually the tax will have to be paid and possibly with penalties.

Those in private practice are scrutinized more carefully than agency employees by the Internal Revenue Service and sometimes by local tax collectors. Because practitioners are paid with many smaller checks and often with cash and they deduct many expenses, tax people sometimes see private practice as an opportunity for avoiding taxes. Because of the extra scrutiny likely to occur, it is essential that well-documented financial recording is accomplished from the beginning.

Private Practice Office

After all the preliminary planning and decision making is done, the worker considers the physical setting for the practice. This consideration is largely based on the kind of clients and practice the practitioner hopes to have. Location and equipment should be appropriate to this target clientele.

Accessibility

The office should be located in a facility that is accessible to clients. Downtown office buildings are ideal settings if the desired clients are mostly professional people but ill-advised for a clientele comprised of children or families who rarely go into the city. If the clientele are economically disadvantaged, mentally ill, or members of the gay community, offices in suburban homes might be unsuitable. But accessibility means more than geography[10]; it also means making clients feel comfortable in the office. If the office has an opulent or formal atmosphere, it might be ideal for older, more affluent couples but might make children, adolescents, or the economically disadvantaged feel ill at ease. If the office has been decorated and equipped in a spartan fashion, it suggests to some potential clients that the worker is not capable of providing the needed service.

Clients will base impressions about the worker on the look of the office as well as on the number of diplomas on the walls, and they are unlikely to avail themselves of the worker's services if the office makes them feel out of place.[11] Therefore, the worker should try to determine in advance the kind of clientele to be served and then locate and decorate accordingly. The practitioner's financial resources and whether the practitioner decides to share facilities may limit choices. The most accessible office possible is basically the best investment.

Possible Settings

Most social workers who enter private practice establish their first offices in their own homes or share offices of more established practitioners. Home and shared offices are especially popular with part-time practitioners because they are convenient, more economical than the alternatives, and often less isolated. More popular with established and full-time practitioners are offices located in commercial buildings and apartment complexes. Some established social workers in private practice have located their offices in detached buildings or converted homes. The advantages of offices in commercial buildings include accessibility to other practitioners and a clientele comprising professionals and the more affluent. Apartment complexes tend to be more homey and provide the practitioner-tenant with many of the amenities available to the residents. In both commercial buildings and apartment complexes, the practitioner can establish a more businesslike and autonomous practice than is possible in the home or shared offices. Owning one's own office in a detached house or condominium has considerable tax advantages for the practitioner and establishes a businesslike atmosphere as well, although the higher costs incurred by purchasing a facility are the major disadvantage of these settings.

Private Offices in Agencies

Many social agencies are now permitting their social work employees the use of agency offices to see private clients after hours. This often salves the wounds of meager pay and benefits and prevents loss of good employees. For the practitioner, this has the advantage of economy and convenience and the disadvantage of little choice about decor, equipment, or variety. This practice is rather new in many social work settings, but disputes have already occurred. NASW's Standards for the Private Practice of Clinical Social Work addresses the issue by recommending

> for private practitioners also employed by an agency, refraining from soliciting or accepting clients for private practice "who have requested services of [the] employer when the employer is able to provide those services."[12]

Home Offices

The home office has the advantage of being less expensive and convenient, and it is immediately available to the worker who wants to get a practice started. The initial investment will not be as great, and the worker can get double duty out of the office by using it for other purposes when no clients are there. The home office usually reflects the worker's tastes, values, and style better than any other possibility and, therefore, can be a very comfortable environment for practice, but the disadvantages are considerable. If the home is located in an area inconvenient for clients, it will be more difficult to attract new referrals. When the home is accessible, the worker possibly loses some sense of privacy. Clients can observe many personal aspects of the worker's life and make judgments based on factors other than practice skills. Privacy is equivocated, and the practitioner cannot avoid bringing work home.

A caution about home offices comes from tax and zoning authorities and landlords. Although it is possible to deduct some of the costs of maintaining a home office from federal and state income taxes, one cannot legally deduct the costs of the entire office. The worker may not claim that the office is used exclusively for the practice unless it is. The worker must keep careful records about household expenses to use in documenting tax claims. Another risk is with possible zoning problems. If the worker's home is in a residential area where businesses are not permitted, difficulties may be encountered. Even if other practitioners have offices in the neighborhood, there is no assurance that permission will always be granted. The other home offices might have been established before the laws that preclude new establishments. Or, the other practitioners might belong to professions that have special permission to have home offices. The worker who wishes to establish a home office should first investigate laws and then get permission from zoning authorities and landlords if necessary.

Physical Amenities

One of the nicest things about private practice is the opportunity to decorate and equip the practice setting to suit one's own taste and pocketbook. In Brett Seabury's study of the physical arrangement of social work offices, he says that private practitioners tend to organize their offices to encourage interaction and to promote feelings of warmth and intimacy.[13] Private practice offices tend to have desks that are not at the center of the room. The focal points are the chairs, usually arranged diagonally to one another, for the worker and the clients. The interview rooms are usually carpeted and contain attractive large plants, tasteful wall hangings, book-filled shelves, and small tables on which lamps are placed. The worker's diplomas and licenses are displayed visibly but not ostentatiously. The setting looks more like a study or a sitting room than a business office. It is obvious that the results of social work intervention are not contingent on the office furniture or arrangements, but these factors do facilitate results and improve the chances of facilitating the worker-client relationship.[14]

Essentials

The minimum requirement for the private practice setting is the practitioner's interview room and a separate waiting room. The walls between the interview and waiting rooms must be soundproof to preserve client confidentiality. If the expense of soundproofing is more than the practitioner can bear at the time, a radio or sound device should be kept on in the waiting room just high enough to mute any sounds coming from the interview room. The waiting clients should have access to a lavatory on or near the premises. If a filing cabinet containing client records is in the waiting room, it should be locked to preserve the safety of the documents. A desk, which can be locked, and a lockable file cabinet are also needed. These safeguard client files as well as any cash payments that have not been deposited.

Office Equipment

The practitioner's office needs little equipment unless the specialization requires toys for work with children. Otherwise, one needs only a telephone with the capability to turn off its ringing and a typewriter. Many workers find it convenient to write out bills in longhand, but typed statements are more professional and businesslike. The typewriter is also needed for the many letters that will be required. The telephone may be in the interview room but should be shut off during the time interviews are being conducted. It is improper to interrupt worker-client sessions whenever the phone rings, and it is inconsiderate to the caller to be talking in front of the client. If the phone has an extension in the receptionist-waiting area, it can be answered there by a secretary or by an answering machine or service.

Answering machines are becoming irritatingly ubiquitous in all walks of life, including private practitioners' offices. However, unless the worker employs a full-time receptionist or an answering service, they are a necessity. The machines, for all their irritability, are inexpensive and convenient, and they protect the worker from interruptions when talking with a client. Their major drawback is that they can be intimidating for many clients, who simply hang up rather than confront an unresponsive voice. A more expensive alternative is the answering service. The worker's phone rings in another office where full-time receptionists take all messages for the worker. This is more personal than a machine, and the client can be more thorough in talking to a person rather than a machine. The disadvantage of the service, in addition to higher costs, is that the operator sometimes receives many calls at once and puts the caller on hold for lengthy periods of time and, if clients hang up on them, the worker is often not informed. Operators can also write down incorrect messages and telephone numbers in their haste.

Office Luxuries

Any other office equipment the worker may want is hardly necessary, and its acquisition may be delayed until the financial position is solid. Such luxuries include reproducing machines, audio or video recorders, postage meters, and computers and computer printers.

The costs of these items are becoming lower and are tax deductible as an office expense if they are used for no other purpose. Their convenience enables the worker to devote more time to professional activities.

Supplies

Essential office supplies should be on hand before the first client is seen. Printed stationery items are the most important and should be ordered two months before seeing clients. Supplies needed include long and short envelopes (plain and with windows), matching letterhead paper, business cards, billing statements, and a book of receipts. All these items are printed with the worker's name, highest academic degree, appropriate designation if incorporated, professional affiliation, practice address, telephone number, and where applicable, professional license numbers. Other important supplies include tissues for tearful clients, manila folders for filing client records, and, perhaps, coffee equipment. Usually these last items are best purchased after the office is opened because they can be procured immediately, and only experience can determine what is essential.

Money Policy

The items described above can be very expensive, and the worker will soon be in financial trouble if income is not forthcoming. Many young private workers think the only problem in meeting overhead and living costs will be to get enough client referrals. Referrals are necessary, but it is not enough to get clients to come; they must also pay for their services. Getting them to do this is more complicated than it seems and requires as much advanced planning as anything else the practitioner does.

Collecting money from clients is often difficult for social workers in private practice. In part, this is because many of them have little practical or theoretical experience, an irony because social work's traditional concern has been to help economically disadvantaged clients provide for their own material needs. Nevertheless, little economic theory is taught in schools of social work.[15] As Eveline Burns, an economist and social work educator, says, little knowledge about economics seems within the social work consciousness.[16]

The social worker in private practice has to change this orientation or change jobs. The worker has to overcome reticence about asking clients to pay for services and must establish a policy about fees and a plan for collection. Before the first client is seen, the worker has to decide how much to charge, how the client is to pay, whether to use a flat rate or sliding scale, whether to charge for missed appointments, and whether to see some clients at no charge.

Informing the Client of Charges

Whatever financial policy, the worker should disclose this information to the client at the first contact. Before the first interview, possibly by phone, letter, or brochure describing the service, the worker must clearly state what the charges will be, the length of the first session, and when and how the fee is to be paid. Otherwise, some clients will expect that there is no charge for the first appointment. They may think the first session is like visiting a contractor, auto mechanic, or lawyer, who gives estimates of the charges when the client eventually contracts for the service. Virtually all helping professionals require the same payment for the first session and those that follow. The first appointment should not be made unless this is clear.

During the first session, the social worker and client should spend a small amount of time discussing the fee system. The client is told how much the cost is for each subsequent session and the procedure and time by which it should be paid. It is useful for the worker to give each client a pamphlet or printed page describing the practitioner's qualifications, methods, and fee system. This further reduces the chances of misunderstanding. It is also helpful to those practitioners who are loath to discuss money with their clients. These workers say nothing that could be construed as crass commercialism, mail bills to the clients, and hope to receive checks by return mail. This attitude is unrealistic, confusing to the client, and can only confound the relationship.

Amount to Charge

The fees that social workers charge vary considerably; there is no legal or professional requirement about the amount to charge. The NASW Code of Ethics simply and clearly states, "When setting fees, the social worker should ensure that they are fair, reasonable, considerate and commensurate with the service performed. . . ."[17] There is ample latitude in this statement, so social workers must look elsewhere when deciding how much to charge. Five factors usually enter into a decision: (1) how much other social workers in the area charge, (2) how much other helping professionals charge, (3) what their own level of experience and education are, (4) what the third-party-financing organizations say are "reasonable and customary charges" for that profession in that area, and (5) what they think will be the most attractive rate to the clientele they hope to attract.

Most social workers set their fees competitively by looking at what other social workers with similar education and experience in their area charge. They also compare the fees charged by other professional groups. In most areas in the United States, ACSW social workers have recently been charging about half the amount charged by local psychiatrists, who have equal experience. This parity is highly influenced by changes in insurance coverages and eligibility, marketplace factors, and the general economy. ACSW social workers charge about 30 percent less than psychologists with Ph.D.s. Social workers with a Ph.D. or DSW and many of those with MSWs and considerable experience charge about the same as psychologists with Ph.D.s. There is widespread variation among practitioners within and between professions, and marketplace conditions often force workers to modify prices up or down after prices have been established.[18]

Third-party organizations are now a major influence in the pricing structure.[19] Health insurance companies keep records of the rates charged by the various local professionals for the services covered. This provides them with the "reasonable and customary" delineation. Practitioners who charge above these limits will not receive reimbursement for the amount beyond the company guidelines.

Charges for Groups and Families

Some workers have different rates for family, couple, and group therapies. A few social workers charge 25 to 50 percent more for an hour with a couple or family than for an hour with an individual, but this is rare. Groups have a very different fee structure. Groups usually are 50 to 100 percent longer than individual sessions, and each group member is charged about half the fee charged by the practitioner for an individual session. For example, if a social worker charged fifty dollars for an individual clinical hour, the charge for each group client would usually be twenty-five to thirty dollars for a session that was 1½ to 2 hours long.

Charges for Nonclinical Services

There is even more variation in the amount charged for nonclinical private practice services. Such services might include consulting for social agencies, providing expert testimony in divorce and custody hearings, leading workshops and providing educational services to profit-making organizations, and writing and calling people in behalf of clients. In part, this is because the health insurance companies do not usually reimburse such activities. Workers usually charge a specified fee for each hour of time spent on such activities. If the worker also engages in clinical practice, the hourly rate is the same as the rates for the clinical hour.

Charging for Special Consideration

Sometimes a social worker might want to charge more than the standard fee to see clients at preferred times or less to see clients at less desirable times. Many clients want sessions in the evenings or on weekends because of their own jobs. This means that the worker sometimes has many hours available at midday but turns people away in the evenings or on Saturdays. However, charging variable fees in this manner is rare and cumbersome; it also raises ethical questions and is of dubious merit among consumer groups.

Fees and Social Work Value Dilemmas

Fee charging raises several value and ethical issues. Among the most debatable of these are the following questions: Should the practitioner set a flat fee for service or use a sliding scale? Should clients be charged for indirect services? Should practitioners provide some services for free? Should the client be charged for missed appointments? Should practitioners ever split fees charged to clients? How can the worker ethically enforce payment of fees?

Flat Rates or Sliding Scales

Social workers in private practice are not in agreement about the preferred method of fee charging. Many feel that it is unethical to vary fees from one client to the next, depending on the client's relative affluence. Other workers feel it is unethical not to use a sliding fee scale because this policy is the only way to remain accessible to the less affluent.[20] The NASW Code of Ethics, in its statement about charges to clients, says fees should be set "with due regard for the clients' ability to pay."[21] To some private practitioners, this is interpreted as requiring workers to scrutinize their clients' finances in order to determine how much should be charged. Others state without equivocation or elaboration that the fixed fee should be applied to all clients.[22]

The trend in private practice is toward the flat fee system for all clients. The consumer movement, the involvement of third-party financial organizations, and workers themselves find too many problems with the sliding fee policy. Consumer groups say it is unethical; many third-party organizations consider it illegal; and many clients and workers find it confusing and unfair.

The social worker who uses a sliding fee scale is not significantly different from a store changing its price on the same item if a customer seems affluent. Consumers of any product or service are entitled to know its price and have some assurance that the price will not change arbitrarily. Social workers who have purchased something only to find the same item on sale the following week know how clients must feel when they pay full rates in a sliding scale practice.

Clients are often not aware of the use of a sliding scale for fees, and when they find out, there can be trouble. The social worker's primary source of new referrals is previous clients, and they will compare information about fees. A former client who paid a full fee may wonder why a newer client is charged less and become dissatisfied. The flexible fee schedule also subjects every client to a "means test," and the worker must spend an inordinate amount of time evaluating the client's resources in order to set the fee. Then the worker has to make periodic reevaluations of the client's fortunes as the treatment progresses. Knowing this, the client might be reluctant to inform the worker of any improvement in finances, because doing so would lead to increased charges. Insurance companies and other third-party organizations find the practice unacceptable; why, they ask, should people be discriminated against through higher charges because they are insured? The principles of equality and fairness are as applicable to those who set fees for private social work practice as they are to anyone.

Free Services

The strong recommendation for fixed fees does not prevent the private practitioner from providing free service on occasion. There are many times in the worker's practice when it is ethically impossible to do otherwise. Clients might begin treatment at the stated fee and then have financial reversals, and it would be unreasonable, if not unethical, to stop their treatment. This often happens when clients divorce during treatment or when children or elderly clients unexpectedly lose their source of support. Then, social workers and other helping professionals have an obligation to arrange for continued service. At the very least, the worker should arrange for the client to begin treatment in a subsidized agency. Many practitioners would continue to see the person for free. Some private practitioners set aside a fixed percentage of their time to see clients free of charge; a waiting list may be established for clients who want those slots. This permits the worker to meet professional and personal obligations to help some disadvantaged people without the aforementioned complications.

Indirect Services

Social workers in private practice have more difficulty with indirect services than do agency workers. Indirect services—those activities that the social worker does on behalf of the client but not necessarily in the client's presence—are a traditional and important component of the social worker's repertoire. For example, the worker may leave the office and meet with members of the client's community, write reports, or give testimony for the client. When the worker is agency-employed, a salary is paid with the understanding that some of the service will be indirect. The private social worker may have difficulty billing clients for such charges unless it is made clear at the outset that indirect service is a possibility and that charges will be based on the time spent in such activity.

Charging for Missed Appointments

The worker must have an established policy about charging a client who has failed to keep a scheduled appointment. If charges are made, it must be known in advance by all clients. Usually, practitioners charge their standard rate unless the client has given ample advance notice of cancellation. Most workers do not charge if the clients notify them of the cancellation at least twenty four hours before the session. The rationale is that the worker has held that time open for the client and will need some time to fill it with another client.

This policy is complicated by third parties. Insurance companies helping to pay for treatment take a dim view of the practice. They tend to refuse reimbursement when they know the charge is for an unkept appointment. In this case, the client must be informed that payment for the session will have to be made without insurance.

The private practitioner can use discretion in implementing the policy. The worker may find it easier to forgive a client who has always been reliable about keeping appointments if he or she has a sudden illness, family emergency, or automobile problem. However, if the client is often absent or seems to be trying to avoid the worker because of an uncomfortable session during the last appointment, the worker might impose the charge.

Group therapy sessions are less flexible. The client is generally charged for every scheduled group session whether he or she is there or not. The only exception some group therapists have to this rule is vacation; clients may miss some meetings if vacations are planned and the group is given ample notice. Otherwise, a group member is charged the full fee for missing a group session, with or without notice. This is because the position in the group is held available to the client; no other person can be added to the group to occupy that position. The group goes on in a person's absence, and, on his or her return, some group time is usually devoted to reviewing what transpired in the client's absence. Here again, some flexibility is in order, but all group clients are entitled to know in advance the policy in effect and any exceptions to it.

Fee-Splitting

An unethical practice that is becoming all too common among private social work practitioners is fee-splitting. This is the practice of referring a client to another professional, who then pays the referring person part of the client's fee. For example, a social worker who wishes to see clients in private practice cannot get referrals; so the worker enters into an arrangement with another practitioner. The practitioner may have an abundance of clients and referral sources and agrees to refer a client for a percentage of the client's payment. Sometimes the established professional is a physician with eligible insurance credentials. Bills to the client and the insurance company are sent in the established practitioner's name, often at higher rates. The social worker in such an arrangement may receive only 50 percent or less of the client's payment.

Some practitioners sign contracts with the established professional in which they agree to treat all those referred at the stated percentage of the client's total fee. The agreement also states that the worker cannot set up his or her own private practice within so many miles of the office of the other professional. This prevents the worker from taking clients if the worker becomes autonomous. The worker who signs such a contract is reducing the possibility of establishing a practice in an area where he or she is well known. But, it must be remembered that this practice is unethical. The NASW Code of Ethics specifically states, "The social worker should not divide a fee or accept or give anything of value for receiving or making a referral."[23]

The practice is also considered unacceptable in the legal, medical, and other professions. It is unethical because it allows practitioners to refer clients not to the professional most suitable for the client's needs but to the person who pays the highest referral fee. The client often has to pay more for the service in order to recover the practitioner's charges.

Despite efforts by the various professions to combat it, the practice is becoming more common. Many who practice it do not consider it to be fee-splitting but a collaborative effort for clients. Others do not think about why it is unethical; all they know is they need the work.

Collaboration

The practice of fee-splitting should not be confused with an effective and desirable approach to service delivery, that of collaboration. The worker who sees clients in a cotherapy situation, on a social work team, or in an interdisciplinary approach is engaged in a perfectly appropriate and ethical practice.[24] Even though both professionals then divide the client fees, there is an important difference from the unethical practice of fee-splitting; the difference is that both practitioners are actively and continuously involved in the treatment.

Charging clients for collaborative treatments may have some complications. Clearly, both practitioners have the right to be paid for their service. Often, each practitioner involved sends a separate bill to the client; in other instances, a single bill with all the collaborators' names on it is sent to the client. Generally, the fee received is divided by the practitioners equally or in proportion to the amount of their time spent with the client.

Payment Policies

Actually, collecting fees from clients is sometimes troublesome. Even though the worker should make the policy about financial obligation clear, there is no assurance that the obligation will always be met. In fact, about 10 percent of all fee-for-service clients do not pay the bills they agreed to pay. This collection ratio is worse for practitioners who are lax about encouraging and enforcing payment. One need not be heartless or obsessed about money collection with clients, but being firm with some clients is certainly in order.

There is little variation in the procedures used by most fee-for-service practitioners. Most professionals mail their bills to clients at the end of each month. It is made known to the client, with a notation on the bill, a sign in the waiting room, or a verbal reminder by the practitioner or secretary, that payment is expected within a specified time period, such as ten days. An increasing number of professionals avoid postage expenses and hand bills to their clients every month. The office secretary may confront the client about payment before or after the session.

Many clients want and expect the practitioner to collect from their insurance company first and then bill them for any remaining amount. This expectation occurs because their family physician and other health care providers follow this method. It is less common in mental health services, however. The insurance companies are slow to reimburse for mental health coverage and slower yet with social workers who are insurance-eligible. If the practitioner agrees to collect from the insurance company first, the client is still asked to bring in and complete insurance forms. If the practitioner does not agree to this condition, the practitioner must tell the client in advance of treatment.

Enforcing Payment

If the client does not pay in the agreed time and manner, the worker has to act promptly and forcefully. The client is asked about payment during the next personal encounter after payment was due. If treatment has concluded and payment has not taken place, the worker may write or call. The monthly statements can also contain messages about late payment; stickers can be attached to these bills warning of consequences. Most clients will pay at some point but some will not, despite all these efforts. Then the worker must simply write it off as a loss or take legal action. The worker can take the matter to a small claims court, engage an attorney, hire a professional bill collector, or use a collection agency (use of a collection agency is the most common of these choices). The worker will find that the other means are very time-consuming and expensive and usually not all that successful. The collection agency takes little time and results in a minimum of unpleasantness, at least for the worker. The disadvantage is that it usually leaves the client with some unattractive thoughts about the worker, but this is an inevitable outcome in any business. It also has the disadvantage that the collector will retain about half the amount collected as a fee for the service.

Flexible Terms

Ethical social workers in private practice are flexible about the terms of payment. They are advised against the sliding fee scale, but they can make the terms of payment very manageable. Agreements can be reached for very low monthly payments spread over many months or years. Most health professionals are not permitted by their ethical codes to charge interest on unpaid balance fees, but many other professionals, such as lawyers and accountants, do. Social work has not established an ethical policy about this as yet; therefore, workers can use their own judgment. Most social workers in private practice do not charge interest on unpaid fees.

In sum, social workers who are careful to plan and prepare for the establishment of their private practices greatly improve the chances that the experience will be worthwhile—for their clients as well as themselves. Having prepared in advance, they can turn their energies to "marketing" their services and building a clientele.

Notes and References

1. C. Rollin Niswonger and Philip Fess, *Accounting Principles* (12th ed.; Cincinnati, Ohio: Southwestern Publishing Co., 1979).

2. See, for example, Clifford Baumback and Kenneth Lawyer, *How to Organize and Operate a Small Business* (7th ed.; Englewood Cliffs, N.J.: Prentice-Hall, 1983); Eugene Brigham, *Financial Management* (2d ed.; Hinsdale, Ill.: Dryden Press, 1979); and *Accounting and Financial Reporting* (Alexandria, Va.: United Way of America, 1979).

3. Internal Revenue Service, *Tax Guide for Small Businesses* (Washington, D.C.: U.S. Government Printing Office, 1984).

4. National Association of Social Workers, "Our Professional Liability Insurance Stands Out," advertisement, *NASW News,* 28 (November 1983), p. 10.

5. Ayala Pines and Ditsa Kafry, "Occupational Tedium in the Social Services," *Social Work,* 23 (November 1978), p. 505.

6. Stephan Levitan and Donald Kornfield, "Clinical and Cost Benefits of Liaison Psychiatry," *American Journal of Psychiatry,* 138 (June 1981), pp. 790–793.

7. Myron Weiner, *Human Services Management: Analysis and Applications* (Homewood, Ill.: Dorsey Press, 1982), pp. 480–481.

8. Martin Goldberg, "To Incorporate or Not To Incorporate: Now It's a Question," *Medical Economics,* December 7, 1981, p. 242.

9. William Grace, *The ABCs of IRAs* (New York: Dell Publishing Co., 1982), pp. 14–26.

10. Ruth Ellen Lindenberg, "Hard to Reach: Client or Casework Agency?" *Social Work,* 3 (October 1958), pp. 23–29.

11. Francis Turner, *Psychosocial Therapy: A Social Work Perspective* (New York: Free Press, 1978), p. 180.

12. National Association of Social Workers, "Council Proposes Definition, Standards for Clinicians," *NASW News,* 28 (May 1983), p. 13.

13. Brett A. Seabury, "Arrangement of Physical Space in Social Work Settings," *Social Work,* 16 (October 1971), pp. 43–49.

14. Lotte Marcus, "Communication Concepts and Principles," in John Turner, ed., *Social Work Treatment: Interlocking Theoretical Approaches* (New York: Free Press, 1979), pp. 409–432.

15. Alfred N. Page, "Economics and Social Work: A Neglected Relationship," *Social Work,* 22 (January 1977), pp. 48–53.

16. Eveline Burns, "Some Economic Aspects of Welfare as an Institution," in John Romanyshyn, ed., *Social Science and Social Welfare* (New York: Council on Social Work Education, 1974), pp. 89–111.

17. National Association of Social Workers, "The NASW Code of Ethics," as cited in Elizabeth Howe, "Public Professions and the Private Model of Professionalism," *Social Work,* 25 (May 1980), p. 186.

18. Robert Barker, *The Business of Psychotherapy: Private Practice Administration for Therapists, Counselors, and Social Workers* (New York: Columbia University Press, 1982).

19. Irene Oppenheimer, "Third-Party Payments," *Social Policy,* 8 (November–December 1977), pp. 55–58.

20. Arthur Goldberg and David Kovac, "A New Concept of Subsidy in Determining Fees for Service," *Social Casework,* 52 (April 1971), pp. 206–219.

21. National Association of Social Workers, "The NASW Code of Ethics," p. 186.

22. Margaret A. Golton, "Private Practice in Social Work," in *Encyclopedia of Social Work*, Vol. 2 (16th issue; New York: National Association of Social Workers, 1971), p. 954.

23. National Association of Social Workers, "The NASW Code of Ethics," p. 186.

24. Robert Barker and Thomas Briggs, *Using Terms to Deliver Social Services* (Syracuse, N.Y.: Syracuse University Press, 1969), pp. 38–39.

6

MARKETING
STRATEGIES

Social workers entering private practice are at a disadvantage compared to many other fee-for-service professionals. They cannot rely on developing a clientele because they are well trained, highly skilled, competent, and honest. They cannot depend on good standing in their profession or their reputation among clients to assure that clients will seek their services. Most people have only vague ideas about why they should seek the services of social workers; social work's function is not yet clear enough to the public, so individual private practitioners have to educate potential consumers and market their services effectively if they are to succeed. Social work has an image problem, which private practitioners have to confront if they are to develop new careers.

Social Work Image

Potential clients obviously do not seek a professional's services unless they understand what services are being offered and believe them to be of value. Usually, a consumer will have a specific idea about which professional or occupational group to consult when they need help. If they want to learn something, they go to a teacher. If they want to sue someone, they consult a lawyer. If someone has a toothache, or a sick dog, or a stopped-up sink, they know whom to consult. The consumer might question whether one or another individual is the best in that field but is less likely to question whether that is the right field. Most people, however, still do not think about seeking the services of a social worker. Many think social work is for someone else, perhaps the poor or the handicapped or only the disadvantaged. Yet people who are poor, handicapped, or disadvantaged do not always look to social work as the profession to take care of their troubles either. When these people have a choice, they want to be served by the same professions who serve the affluent or nondisadvantaged or nonhandicapped. This should be self-evident.

Because of the vague image, many private practitioners avoid identifying themselves to potential consumers as a social worker. This is unfortunate for the profession, the client, and the practitioner, but like it or not, it occurs for a reason. Dale Hardman uses his delightful writing style to chide private practitioners who do not identify their profession on their shingles and stationery. "Tell me, Mr. Pringle," writes Hardman, "don't you consider social work an honorable profession?. . .Then for some reason are you ashamed of being identified with the profession? Low status, perhaps?"[1]

The number of practitioners who still avoid the social work designation is unknown. In 1955, Helen Perlman estimated that there were very few, if any, private practitioners who acknowledged their social work roots. "To my knowledge," she wrote, "the title is never used by [the private practitioner trained in social work] as his professional designation. It may have too little meaning for his prospective clients—or too much."[2] If this estimate was true in 1955, it is certainly not true now. One need only look in the telephone book's yellow pages under "Social Workers" to see that many practitioners have no problem with the designation. However, one is likely to see even more social workers listed elsewhere in the same book under "Marriage Counselors," "Psychotherapists," "Group Therapists," and "Family Mediators," among many other designations.

Why are not all social workers, like practitioners in other disciplines, unreservedly eager to display their professional identity? One of the most influential private practitioners, Arnold Levin, who once chaired an NASW Committee on Private Practice, offered one answer. He has downplayed the title for himself and wrote that he could not recommend that anyone in private practice use the label of social worker, at least not without further description. He believes that, for most people, the designation brings to mind the "image of a public assistance, bureaucratic functionary shuffling papers, interpreting rules and regulations, and guarding or disbursing the taxpayers' moneys in miserly amounts."[3] Another possible answer was provided by a private practitioner who wrote to the author: "I list my professional affiliation as 'social worker' but not with enthusiasm. It simply isn't a good way to draw clientele. The public doesn't know what social workers do. I have to be more specific about the work I do. My name and MSW degree are right on my door and below that is 'psychiatric social worker.' But I also put 'psychotherapist' on that door. People know what a psychotherapist does." Another social worker in full-time private practice wrote: "People don't think they should have to pay a social worker much for his services. So I guess it's a financial thing. But it's more too. A lot of doctors and lawyers would refer someone to a psychologist or a teacher or a physical therapist, but they don't have the foggiest notion of what a social worker is so they aren't going to refer anyone to them."

However, this is not to suggest that the designation "social worker" is a liability in private practice. An increasing number of studies about the public's perception of social work shows that the profession is viewed more favorably than ever before.[4] Although the profession might have been held in low regard by the majority of the public at one time, this is no longer true. Most people feel indifferent about it at worst, for they do not have a clear understanding of what it is. Social work is still trying to define its specific domain and expertise to its own members.[5] If the members are not yet clear, one can hardly expect the public to be. As long as social work is ill-defined to the public, the private practitioner cannot consider membership in social work to be as great an asset in building a clientele as do other professionals in their own professions. Thus, the private practitioner's concern should not be that the "social work" appellation will lose business, but only that it may not bring any.

In sum, to achieve a successful private practice, social workers have to market their services rather than rely on their profession—or the public's perception of their profession—to do it for them.[6] They have to learn to tailor marketing strategies on an individual basis in order to attract consumers.

Specializing

Perhaps the most common and successful marketing strategy used by private practitioners is specialization. The practitioner tells the public that he or she is a social worker who works with certain target populations or uses specific treatment methods. For example, all social workers are familiar with the experience of introducing themselves to strangers and saying, "I'm a social worker," only to be met with polite nods and blank stares. People are probably not being unfriendly, but, because they are vague about the role of social work, they just do not know how to respond. However, if the social worker said instead, "I'm a social worker in private practice. I specialize in working with teenagers who have alcohol or drug abuse problems," the worker would be remembered. Then, if an individual later came into contact with an adolescent addict, the meeting with the social worker would be likely to come to mind. The person may become a referral source. Practitioners can get their names and special areas of expertise firmly intertwined in the minds of the referring public, and whenever anyone thinks of a kind of problem or methodology, they may think of a specific social worker.

Unfortunately, some social workers will view the private practitioner's effort to specialize as being disloyal to the profession. They might see the practice as a guise to disavow one's social work identity by becoming too focused. Some workers are "weeping for the lost profession" because of a possible trend toward specialization.[7] This view is understandable even if debatable. The distinctiveness of social work, and its proudest tradition, has always been its determination to see the "big picture." Its expansive and generic approach to social problems and its goal of enhancing the well-being of people in society are noble, but it is unrealistic to think that one person can do everything well. Some social workers are better suited to being generalists, while others make better specialists. It is no more disloyal to be one than the other. The profession has room for both.

Once social workers have become identified with a speciality, it becomes easier to promote themselves to potential consumers. Once the specialty is defined, the promotion techniques used by the private social work practitioner are quite similar to the techniques used by other professions in private practice as well as those used by many other businesses. Private practitioners must make clear to the public what it is that they are selling and that the product or service is attractive and worthwhile, and that their particular product or service is competitive with similar offerings of others. Social workers should make the service convenient and accessible to the potential consumer. Finally, they can build a reputation for honesty and quality of goods or service by satisfying the consumer. This leads to return business and word-of-mouth recommendations. These techniques are the foundation of any reputable business.

Referrals

Surveys showing the origin of private practice referrals are consistent. Most private practitioners get referrals (in order of importance) from former clients, physicians, social agency staff members, self-referrals, psychiatrists and psychologists who seek social services in collaboration with their own cases, lawyers, school counselors, the clergy, and miscellaneous others.[8]

Sources

The most important source of referral is, of course, a satisfied client and people close to the client. The client who is happy with the outcome of work with the professional is the best advertisement there can be. Many of the client's associates who know about the contact with the social worker are also going to become "advertisers," if not clients themselves. The second most important referral source is physicians, who care about their patients but do not always have sufficient time, skill, or inclination to meet their social service and mental health care needs. It is true physicians are more likely to refer their patients to psychiatrists because they are more familiar with the techniques of fellow medical doctors. However, when they have first-hand knowledge of social work and the techniques used, they are more likely to send their patients to a social worker. Private practitioners can readily demonstrate to physicians that their training, experience, and skill are focused toward helping people with family, marital, and social relationship problems than is true of most psychiatrists. The first referrals from the doctor to the social worker will probably be followed very carefully; if the results are poor or even equivocal, the doctor will be reluctant to make additional referrals.

The staffs of social agencies, especially if the worker was related to the agency before entry into private practice, are the third most important referral source. For many social workers entering private work, this is a major, if not only, source. Private practitioners sometimes get an agency's "client overload," or at least get their names on the list of the agency's referral resources for those clients whom the agency cannot serve. Many social workers keep in close contact with several agencies for this purpose. Again, such efforts will only be effective in the long run when workers provide competent service.

Psychiatrists, psychologists, lawyers, school counselors, and the clergy can also be important referral sources for social workers. However, referrals come from them only in certain cases. These professionals will probably refer only if they know the worker directly, or know the worker's special expertise indirectly. They must see the worker as offering some unique skill or knowledge and some form of treatment that does not duplicate the services other professionals provide. Social workers must also show that they are ethical and competent. When social workers target members of these professions as potential referral sources, they usually find it effective to cultivate a personal or working relationship in activities of mutual interest. It is always more effective to show one's competence than simply to claim it.

Referral-Building Activities

Whatever the referral sources, the chances for referral increase if the worker is known personally or because of expertise. Thus, the fundamental referral-building activity consists of becoming known by those who may recommend clients. Private practitioners have concentrated on six basic activities to accomplish this: (1) communicating with those who have already made referrals, (2) careful follow-up on former clients and referrers, (3) contacting those who have not referred clients but who have a professional interest in a client, (4) "prospecting" for clients, (5) advertising, and (6) participating in community activities. Of course, not all private practitioners are involved in all these activities or even approve of their colleagues who do.

Communicating with Referrers. By far the most important way to become known by referrers is to communicate with them. The first communication occurs as soon as the worker learns that someone has made the referral. The referral is acknowledged by phone or letter when the potential client contacts the worker. A brief note on the worker's stationery might simply say, "Thank you for recommending my services to Mrs. ——. She called for an appointment today, and we will meet on ——. With her permission, I will keep you informed about the findings and recommendations."

After the assessment is completed, if the client gives permission, a more complete letter is sent to the referrer. If the referrer is a professional, such as the family physician, the letter may include a summary of the presenting problem, the social work assessment, the recommended treatment, the prognosis, and the worker's plan for helping to solve the problem. If the practitioner plans to continue working with the client, the letter concludes by saying that subsequent progress notes will be sent. If the letter goes to the physician, it is marked at the top, "CONFIDENTIAL: FOR FILE ONLY." The letter is usually kept in the physician's file on the patient, so the worker's name and telephone number are available thereafter. As treatment continues, less formal and less detailed progress notes may be sent. They might say: "Mrs. —— has been attending our weekly group therapy sessions regularly. She seems motivated and appears to be progressing. I'll notify you if there are any changes. Again, thank you for recommending me to her."

When the goals of the intervention are reached or when termination takes place, the referrer is given a more detailed summary. A letter, again marked "CONFIDENTIAL: FOR FILE," summarizes the intervention process and indicates which goals have been reached and which have not. It includes a prognosis and indicates what to look for in the future in case some regression occurs. The letter also indicates that the worker will continue to keep in touch with the client and concludes with another "thanks for the referral."

If the referral source is not a professional but a personal acquaintance or family member, there are significant differences in the way communication takes place. Usually a brief informal note or call saying the person made the contact is enough. It is, of course, inappropriate to provide any substantive information to such persons about the nature of the problem or intervention plan. They do deserve, however, the courtesy of acknowledging their effort.

The client must always give permission before any substantive information is sent. Clients are usually amenable to this communication, and some even expect it. Many private practitioners find it useful to let clients read any information to be sent out so that changes can be made in advance. In such cases, the client might be asked to initial the copy kept in the worker's file to indicate that approval of the communication took place. If more detailed information is requested by relevant others, it is essential to get the client to sign a written release of information form.

There are many advantages to communicating in this way. Most important, it provides some coordination between those who are trying to help the client. It is consistent with the social work orientation of involvement in the client's environment and it minimizes problems that can occur with referrers who might want to stay involved in the intervention process or second-guess the worker's efforts with the client.[9] The more these others are kept informed and made to feel a part of the helping process, the less they will interfere. Finally, communication keeps the social worker in the mind of the referrer. Showing that the worker is conscientious, organized, and can work on a plan to reach a goal does a great deal to improve the chances of subsequent referrals.

Follow-up Activities. Clients who never again hear from their worker may feel the worker is not interested in them or they may forget the successful results they had achieved during their treatment. It is almost always worthwhile for private practitioners to stay in some contact with clients who have terminated. The worker might occasionally call or write a brief note. A handwritten note on office stationery might say something like: "It's been over a year since we last met, and I was just thinking about you. I hope all remains well with you and your family." The worker can also do this with the source of referral, indicating that there has been no word from the client for many months and the worker was hoping that all was well. In both instances, it demonstrates continued interest, is professional, and is a reminder that the worker is still there. The client remembers the worker and is aware that the worker is still in practice. This does not suggest, however, that the worker should become part of the client's life outside treatment. There may be times when the former client might want to invite the worker to parties or to see him or her socially. The worker would be unwise to have any such involvement; the basis of the relationship was, and always shall be, the client's therapeutic interests, and any socializing, regardless of how long after termination, is dubious practice.

Contact with Relevant Others. A way some private practitioners meet potential referrers is by contacting them about or in behalf of existing clients. For example, if a client is referred by friends, the worker may ask the new client the name of his or her physician. Then, with permission, the worker writes to the doctor, saying that the client is being seen. A letter can indicate who referred the client and for what reason. It can have a sentence or two stating the worker's qualifications for seeing the client, then it can present the social work assessment, prognosis, and intervention plan. The worker may also promise to keep the physician informed about the client's progress. When goals are reached, a final summary letter is sent. At this point, the procedure is the same as communicating with a referring physician. This procedure is appropriate for many professionals in the client's helping network: If the client is having some educational difficulties, school counselors may be contacted; if there are marital problems, the client's clergy may be notified; if some potential conflict about financial problems or legal difficulties seems relevant, a letter might go to the client's attorney. Clients often appreciate this kind of attention and easily give permission for such contacts to be made. Nevertheless, it should not be done unless the client gives permission, and, in most cases, it is advisable to let the client read and initial any letters first. This way, no information goes out that the client wants concealed.

This activity is beneficial to all concerned. The client has more input with those in the helping network, and the professional community is informed about the intervention. The worker becomes known to those who had been unaware of the worker's existence or professional expertise. The worker is seen as one who is concerned about clients and capable of recognizing the client's problem and providing appropriate service to correct it. It is consistent with social work values and norms, for it shows that the worker does not see clients existing in a vacuum or only in a clinical setting completely detached from external or environmental considerations. Practically, it enhances the chances of referrals from new sources.

These techniques for building a clientele asume that the worker already has some clients and can build a practice and caseload on

this foundation. Workers who have no clients at all, and thus have
no foundation on which to build a practice, are more likely to rely
on prospecting, advertising, and community activities. Many professionals have very negative feelings about the first two, but virtually
everyone feels positive about the appropriate use of the third.

Prospecting for Clients. Many business people call on potential
customers at random in the hope that a percentage of those contacted will use their services or products. For example, insurance
and real estate salespeople call or knock on doors looking for potential customers. Some lawyers appear at accidents, dispensing their
business cards to offer their services.

Most professional people who attempt to get referrals by the "prospecting" process, however, use more subtle techniques. A common
and acceptable form is to send out announcements and letters of
introduction to those who might become referral sources. Announcements are typically 3 × 5 inch printed pasteboard cards that say
something like: "Sylvia Lee, ACSW, DSW, announces the opening
of her office for the practice of social work treatment of children
and adolescents." The address and available hours are also indicated.
The cards, while traditional, are not very effective by themselves.
Few professionals are likely to refer clients to someone they do not
know, and especially not to someone whose profession is not well
known to them. If cards have any worth at all, it is as part of a
whole procedure for becoming known to referral sources. They will
be forgotten unless they are soon followed by additional contacts.

Another procedure, perhaps one that follows the announcement
card, is the letter of introduction. This letter would be useless, or
perhaps harmful, as an impersonal form letter. It should be written specifically for the addressee and call attention to mutual interests, concerns, and goals. It should not solicit referrals. It merely
says that the social worker is opening a private practice in the area
and will specialize in working with certain kinds of problems or
client groups. It will briefly state the worker's credentials and
experience. The letters are also not very effective, unless some additional contact is made soon after they are received. Ideally, the contact is in the form of a personal contact or a message about a client
who has started to work with the social worker.

Some workers prefer a personal follow-up. They state in their letter of introduction that they might informally drop in at the addressee's office in the near future. A few days after the letter of introduction or announcement card is sent, they go to the office, talk with the receptionist, ask if the employer is available to say hello. If the professional is unavailable, the worker can simply leave a card and more information about his or her practice and background. It is unwise to take more than a few minutes with the contact, for it indicates that the worker has nothing better to do than visit. It is also unwise to schedule a formal meeting; this can be an irritating intrusion, and the worker would have to be very clear about the nature of the call or take the chance of being billed for the time.

Advertising. Many private practitioners now see merit in advertising as a way to reach initial referrals, although others still find the practice abhorrent. The conflict about advertising exists among all fee-for-service professionals. For the past century, the practice had been considered unethical because of the abuses that had been rampant in the nineteenth century, in which practitioners would make unsubstantiated claims to attract clientele. Reputable professions could only combat this by keeping members from advertising. Their premise was that clients would get to the practitioners by referrals from other reputable professionals or not at all. However, the consumer movement and the Federal Trade Commission regulations took a different stance in the 1960s; then, the professional organizations that forbade their members from advertising were seen as attempting to restrict fair trade and uphold high fees. Now it is illegal for any profession to prevent members from advertising, and ads in the media for lawyers, doctors, dentists, accountants, and social workers have become commonplace. Relevant professional associations now try to provide assurance that the advertised claims are truthful and reflect the member's integrity and that of the profession.

Whether or not the private practitioner should advertise is now an individual decision rather than a professional one. There are many advantages and disadvantages for each practitioner. Ads can clarify for the public what the social worker is qualified to do and interested in doing for potential clients and what the charges are. Because social work's role and expertise are not that well known to the public, this can be an important equalizer. On the other hand, professionals who do not advertise often have an unfavorable impression of those who do, and they are not likely to become referral sources.

Advertising may also not be cost effective. It is expensive, and the well-established worker does not really need to reach more than a few new clients each month in order to maintain a full caseload. The newer professional will find it cost-inefficient at best, unless it is pinpointed to specific target groups. Without a chain of offices and employees, it is pointless to advertise in those places where large numbers of people are reached or far beyond the location of the practitioner's office.

One of the most common methods used by practitoners for notifying potential clients is through the Yellow Pages.[10] It is not usually necessary or effective for the social worker to purchase a large display ad in these pages, no matter what the claims about its effectiveness. In the helping professions, the Yellow Page listing is considered a supplement to various forms of public exposure; it is a way to let clients who have heard about the worker find a telephone number. Therefore, a simple line or two is sufficient.

However, if the worker feels dependent on listings in the Yellow Pages, arrangements for inclusion should be made well in advance of entry into private practice. The telephone company has deadlines for new listings of about six months prior to publication of each book, so a worker who just misses a deadline could have to wait as long as one and a half years before the listing could appear. To avert this, workers can notify the telephone company as soon as they know they are going to enter private practice. They can first use a home phone number and then, when their office and business phones are established, have the telephone company record a change of number announcement. Thus, whenever clients call using the listed number, they can still get the worker.

Under what Yellow Page heading is the best place to be included? Many practitioners choose to be listed under "Marital and Family Counselors," "Consultants," "Psychotherapists," or "Guidance Clinics," if it is legal in that jurisdiction. They believe that few people will look up "Social Worker" when they have a problem. Nevertheless, the practitioner should also be listed under "Social Workers." As workers become known to clients, referral sources, and third-party financers, their numbers and addresses will be sought in that listing.

The Yellow Pages as well as other forms of advertising are impersonal, and the referral sources and potential clients will be more attracted to seeking those practitioners about whom they have had previous contact or knowledge. Ads should be considered no more than a supplement to activities designed to keep the practitioner in the public eye. They will always be more costly and less effective than community activities. Relating to the public is the private practitioner's best single means of getting new referrals.

Referral Building through Community Activity. Social workers, more than any other professional group, are supposed to be involved in the community and in its resources. They are supposed to be aware of the consequences of social problems affecting individuals and are oriented to changing those problems as well as personal problems. Private practice does not excuse a social worker from this responsibility. Even if it did, there are many rewards for such involvement. It is an effective way for the worker to practice social work ideals and help people at levels of intervention different from the treatment model. Practically speaking, it is an excellent way for the social worker to get into the public eye and into the consciousness of those who might seek the worker's services or those who might refer people who do. To achieve these goals, seven community activities in which workers have been engaged have been identified as being particularly effective.[11] They are discussed below.

1. *Providing free consultations.* One community activity is offering services to one or more social agencies or self-help groups as a free consultant. Such organizations abound, and they often have little money to pay for professional advice. Many social agencies are now struggling to keep afloat because they have serious financial problems; they are increasingly staffed by volunteers or less well-trained professionals. To retain their credibility and maintain their valuable public services, they require (but can ill-afford) professional expertise. Self-help groups are also grateful for the occasional input they get from professionals, but they have scant resources to hire them. If the private practitioner met periodically with such agencies and groups in order to answer questions or provide feedback, the time spent would be mutually rewarding.[12] Such contacts would help the worker "keep on his/her toes" as well as help to refine skills and increase knowledge. Contacts with others outside the isolation of the office would also help reduce vulnerability to burnout. And,

of course, the exposure would make the worker known to a larger group of potential referrers.

2. *Serving on agency boards.* Those agencies that are better funded and more formally organized need community leaders to serve on their boards. A board determines an agency's policy and oversees its functions as well as determines its priorities. Social workers often take on such roles, and they have much to offer in such capacities. They can interpret for their fellow board members the ethical and value bases for actions taken by agency staffs. They can help set agency policy in ways more consistent with social work values and orientations. Agency workers seldom are able to do this, as they are ineligible for serving on their agency's board, but private social workers are in an ideal position to serve. The private practitioner is an indigenous member of the community who is aware of the needs of the agency as well as the community. On the board, the practitioner often works with members of other professions, including doctors, lawyers, clergy, and business leaders, affording ample opportunity for a demonstration of knowledge and skill. The worker's fellow board members often become referral resources, as do agency staff members.

3. *Public speaking.* Social workers only need to hint at their willingness to speak before civic groups, educational associations, church meetings, and fraternal organizations to be given the opportunity. Almost every organization has regular formal programs in which the membership is eager to learn about a community problem or professional solution to a problem. If the worker proves to be informative and interesting for the group, other groups will hear about it and extend invitations as well. In these talks, the worker might show an interest and knowledge about an issue that is of particular concern to the group. The worker might describe how professionals address such problems and provide many examples of the activity. This helps the audience to identify the speaker as one who might provide such services on a fee-for-service basis. Some members of the audience might think about using the worker's services, or they will know of others who might benefit from it.

4. *Panel discussions.* A similar but less demanding activity that accomplishes results similar to public speaking is to participate in panel discussions or act as a resource person for community workshops. Letting groups know of an interest in being a discussant at

a formal speech made by another professional will lead to invitations. The worker's credentials are usually described, and he or she is called upon as an expert. Panel discussions are less structured and formal situations than are speech presentations, so it is easy for the worker to mingle with the audience during the course of the evening and to be seen by members of the group as one who might be able to help. It is not at all uncommon for workers to receive telephone calls following these presentations from someone who attended the meeting and wants an appointment.

5. *Campaigns.* There are two parts to this activity, and they are not for every social worker in private practice; however, those who engage in them find considerable public exposure. One part is to campaign for and hold elective office; the other is to lead or participate in public crusades to change some social norm or law. Social workers are often encouraged to become more political. This is not always possible for those who work in publicly funded social agencies that frown on certain political activities. The private practitioner is under no such constraints and, in fact, should be in a very good position for such activities. Social workers are as well qualified as other professionals to administer public programs and set public policy. Even if they do not win the election or accomplish the cause they fought for, the workers have still established themselves as leaders in the community and, as such, are in a better position to influence the community, teach others, and gain referrals. If they are successful in the effort, their private practice experience can be helpful in their roles as administrators and business leaders.

6. *Media involvement.* The last activity is designed to reach the public through the media, and there are a number of possible approaches that can be used. One approach is appearing on local radio or television programs. Public interest programs abound on all stations (they are required by the Federal Communications Commission), and the hours are necessarily filled by people who have something to say. Problems in the community of interest to a specific segment of the population are often the subjects of concern. If the worker is able to speak clearly, with some humor and irreverence and in a jargon-free way, the worker will be welcome on many of these programs. The worker then has a vehicle for expressing concern, interest, and skill in dealing with the problem under discus-

sion. Identified on the program as a local private practitioner who works with the specific problem, the worker is likely to be called by some listeners who seek additional advice.

Practitioners can accomplish something of the same thing by writing articles and columns for newspapers and magazines. Often these works are in the form of advice-giving columns using question-and-answer formats. The larger magazines and newspapers usually have professionals who write such material and are not inclined to print much from new private practitioners, but there are numerous neighborhood newspapers, advertising flyers, newsletters, and other printed matter where the practitioner can find a vehicle for this form of expression. Workers can also call attention to themselves, their views, and their skills by writing letters to the editor to discuss matters of their own concern or special skills when such issues have already been mentioned in the paper. The worker describes what is right and wrong about a published article and thus receives some more public attention as a specialist.

Writing for professional journals is another way of expanding the referral base. Even though the article is addressed to the professional community, other professionals in the area will take the writer more seriously as an expert. It can lead to contacts with other professionals and thus to the possibility of more referrals. This happens especially when the journal appeals to members of more than a single profession.

7. *Role modeling.* The last possibility for expanding the referral base is the most important. It is to present one's self in a positive, ethical, and knowledgeable way to whatever public sector is being addressed. All the public relations activities one can think of are fruitless if the worker is dishonest or engages in behaviors that discredit the individual or the profession. If ethical business practices are performed at all times and if the worker is a good citizen, it is worth all the other public relations activities put together.

Clearly, the worker cannot engage in all these community relations activities, or there would be no time to work with fee-paying clients. It is equally clear that the private social work practitioner will find it necessary and useful to engage in some of them. The vague image of the profession requires that the individual worker in private practice communicate with the public to clarify individual skills as well as those of the profession. Some workers are obviously not well equipped to participate in one or another of these activities, but there are enough possibilities that some will appeal to any private practitioner. Each worker has the opportunity to choose those that might be most useful and effective, given the particular personality, expertise, and community.

Notes and References

1. Dale G. Hardman, "Mr. Pringle's Shingle," *Social Work,* 23 (January 1978), p. 4.

2. Helen Perlman et al., "Psychotherapy and Counseling," *Annals of the New York Academy of Sciences,* 63 (1955), pp. 319–432.

3. Arnold M. Levin, "Private Practice Is Alive and Well," *Social Work,* 21 (September 1976), p. 361.

4. C. David Condie et al., "How the Public Views Social Work," *Social Work,* 23 (January 1978), pp. 47–53.

5. Jona M. Rosenfeld, "The Domain and Expertise of Social Work: A Conceptualization," *Social Work,* 28 (May–June 1983), pp. 186–191.

6. Mark H. Lewin, "Learning to Market Services," *Professional Psychology,* 7 (May 1976), pp. 243–245.

7. Judith Lee, "Weeping for the Lost Profession: Social Work in Transition," *Jewish Social Work Forum,* 19 (Spring 1983), pp. 20–32.

8. Robert L. Barker, *The Business of Psychotherapy: Private Practice Administration for Therapists, Counselors, and Social Workers* (New York: Columbia University Press, 1982), pp. 142–148.

9. Mara Selvini-Palazzoli et al., "The Problem of the Referring Person," *Journal of Marital and Family Therapy,* 6 (January 1980), pp. 3–10.

10. James Allison and Klaus Hartman, "A Note on Choosing a Service Provider from Telephone Listings," *Journal of Counseling Psychology,* 9 (January 1981), pp. 78–80.

11. Barker, *The Business of Psychotherapy,* pp. 163–168.

12. Ronald W. Toseland and Lynda Hacker, "Self-Help Groups and Professional Involvement," *Social Work,* 27 (July 1982), pp. 341–347.

7

OUTLOOK FOR PRIVATE PRACTICE

This book began with a glimpse of the past, of the inauspicious, bastardlike origins of private practice, whose social work parents wanted to disown it, whose growth continued without much nurture or guidance, but whose size and influence now make it hard to disavow. It will end with a look at the future, at a time when private practice will enter a promising maturity and its social work progenitor will be enfeebled by decreased public support for the programs, methods, and agencies that had once been the reason for existence. As Arnold Levin succinctly put it, "Private practice is alive and well, but the profession of social work may not be."[1]

One needs reminding, however, that social work has overcome considerable adversity many times in the past, while private practice has not yet had to prove its durability. Private practice might appear strong and vital to some, but it has three serious vulnerabilities, any one of which could lead to its premature senescence or demise. Private practice in social work is vulnerable because of changing social and economic conditions, decreased support from third-party organizations, and problems within the social work profession itself. The degree to which the profession solves or circumvents these problems will largely determine the fate of its private practice.

Socioeconomic Vulnerabilities

The growth of private practice in the past two decades was largely due to favorable economic conditions. An increasing number of consumers wanted the service, and the national economy was relatively healthy; so more people could afford to pay for it. Many people who

had no serious emotional or social problems simply wanted to understand themselves better. There was a shortage of professional providers in agencies, and the agencies had long waiting lists. Government programs and insurance companies were more willing and able
to help pay for the service.

Obviously, private practice would not be economically vulnerable
if such conditions continued indefinitely, but change is the nature
of the economic climate. Every factor that once encouraged the
growth of private practice is currently undergoing transformation.

For example, there is now evidence that the demand for the services of private practitioners in all helping professions has peaked
and is in decline.[2] This is true because of changing demographics,
value priorities, and cost factors. Demographically, there are fewer
people in the age categories that were traditionally the most likely
consumers of the service. Within this smaller pool of potential
clients, fewer people now seek most forms of psychosocial therapy
services. A decade ago, demand for service was reaching fadlike pro-
portions with some groups. Those who went to therapists and social
workers were not only the people with serious mental illnesses or
social dysfunction problems; many went to enhance their potential
as human beings, to become self-actualized, or to gratify narcissis-
tic impulses.[3] Far fewer people now see psychotherapy or psychosocial intervention as the primary device by which to achieve such
objectives. The value and efficacy of therapy and social services in
private practice has still not been clearly demonstrated to the public
or to third parties who help pay the bills.[4] Finally, costs have become
an even greater obstacle to many. Prices stay high even during reces-
sions and even with increased professional competition. Costs were
not important to consumers when their insurance companies and
government programs paid most of the service provider's charges,
but third parties have been reducing mental health care coverage,
making the costs prohibitive for many.

Even though demand has slackened, the supply of mental health
care workers continues to grow. There are now over one million
Americans who provide some form of counseling, guidance, or therapy to other Americans or to each other.[5] Many new professions have
recently emerged to provide even more "therapy," and older professions are expanding their memberships to do likewise. People with

no formal training and those with dubious credentials are also hanging out their shingles in unprecedented numbers. Some professions, including medicine, have declared that they have too many members and have taken corrective actions.[6] Physicians, for example, have made it more difficult for students to enter their professional schools and have successfully lobbied to keep graduates in foreign professional schools from practicing in the United States. The supply-demand imbalance has caused some professional associations to intensify their competitive efforts against other groups. In several states, professional associations testified against various groups who sought to be licensed as professional mental health care providers. Many professions are now campaigning vigorously to retain their own eligibility for reimbursement with insurance companies while seeking to exclude other groups.[7]

Third-Party Vulnerabilities

Insurance companies and other third-party institutions constitute a significant risk for private practitioners. Third parties still pay for most of the mental health care offered in private practice. While funding has made therapy more accessible, it has also influenced choices about which helping methods and professional groups will survive. If insurance companies reimbursed all professional groups on an equal basis, using the same criteria for all, or if they did not reimburse any outpatient mental health care providers, then consumers would choose for themselves which services and providers they would seek. No doubt social work, or at least its most effective practitioners, could hold their own and compete effectively, but when an insurance company says it will help pay for services rendered only by members of designated professions or for specified forms of treatment, those excluded will be at a competitive disadvantage, no matter how worthwhile their work.[8]

Social work's position with the insurance companies is precarious. Even though many political leaders such as Senator Daniel Inouye from Hawaii have strongly advocated including the profession in third-party reimbursement plans, the opposition is considerable.[9] It comes from many of the insurance companies themselves as well as from competing professional groups.

Many insurance companies are increasingly reluctant to reimburse social workers. They argue that with fewer providers, there will be fewer claims that they will have to pay.[10] This would reduce their costs and increase their profitability. Social work is a prime candidate for exclusion because its educational requirements are lower than those in other fields and because its quality control provisions may seem less rigorous than in other professions. Third parties also see many of the services that social workers provide as being outside the realm of their responsibility. They clearly say their role is with individual health problems. While they have been begrudging and discriminatory about paying for mental health care compared with physical health care, they are adamant against paying for prevention or the kind of indirect and social relationship services that are the social worker's forte.[11] Social work, justifiably proud of its person-in-environment perspective, finds it hard to justify to insurance companies that they should pay for such interventions. It is not enough for social work to be right about the broader orientation; it has the formidable task of convincing insurance companies that it is right and cost-effective.[12] Otherwise, to remain competitive with other professional groups, it would have to narrow its approach.

Another problem developing with third parties is their growing participation in "preferred provider organizations." Private medical practitioners concerned about the surplus of providers and insurance companies concerned about escalating costs are uniting to form these organizations all over the nation.[13] Hospitals or groups of physicians contract with insurance companies and government reimbursing agencies to provide lower "group rates" for those insured. The physicians agree to provide care to certain insured people, say all policy holders who work for a particular company, for the lower fee. The PPO group also agrees to hold down questionable medical services. The insurance company agrees to channel more patients to them. Their policy holders can still go to the provider of their choice, but those who choose a PPO physician pay lower rates and have better deductibles and copayments. PPOs are seen by some as private medical practice's answer to the growing pressure from competing professional groups and from prepaid medicine such as Health Maintenance Organizations (HMOs). With their advent, insurance companies may be even less willing to reimburse those providers who are not members.[14] Thus far, there is little to indicate that the doctors who develop PPOs are inclined to include many social workers and other nonpsychiatric mental health care providers in their ranks; including too many people would defeat the purpose.

Private practitioners cannot, by themselves, prevent their exclusion from third-party reimbursement. The efforts they make as individuals toward this end can only be futile. No company would exclude an entire profession while making an exception for one specific practitioner. Private social workers can only hope for a solution through a unified effort made by their professional association. If the profession remains vital and resolved to show that social work in private practice is of value, then there is a reasonable chance that third parties will be convinced.

Professional Vulnerabilities

The following scenario illustrates the professional sources of vulnerability faced by many in private practice: It is the near future in a Midwestern state. The legislature is debating whether or not to license social workers. It had voted down the proposal twice, but the lobbyists have been persistent. Finally, one senator rises and says, "I'm against this proposal. Social work doesn't do anything that isn't done by many other professional groups. No one has to take a test to prove they are competent in this state. They say this is because they haven't come up with a test that proves who can and who can't do social work. NASW has a test, but not every social worker in this state has to take it. None of the older social workers have to take it anywhere. And they don't have to prove that they are keeping up-to-date. Why should this state license a group like that?"

The legislature once again rejects the proposal. On the basis of that action, the state's insurance companies and government agencies announce they will not reimburse for social work services. Agency social workers are irritated but go about their work. Private practitioners are much more upset. They try to hold on, seeing clients who do not require third-party payments. They work harder as individuals to show that they are competent, but the handwriting is on the wall. Most of them cannot survive as private practitioners unless they become affiliated with professions that are eligible for third-party payment. Many go back to agency work if they can find jobs. Some leave social work and enter new occupations altogether. Some return to school to become educated in fields that are eligible for payments. Many move to states that have licensing.

Some decide to form a new organization made up exclusively of private practitioners. They develop difficult, highly specialized entrance examinations and give them to all social workers who want to take them. They define their practice in very specific terms. They establish a rigorous peer review mechanism, a continuing education system without grandfathering, and a plan to get licensing in the state just for the small group. As a group that provides a very focused, unique, and definable service, the prospects for licensing are favorable.

The new group is denounced by other social workers as being too narrow, too selfish, and too myopic to see the broader needs of society. They are isolated from social work and eventually come to think of themselves as something different. They decide to call themselves by another name. They consider such designations as "mediation specialists," "ombudsmen," "familyologists," "societrists," "social dysfunction specialists," "communicationists," "caseworkers," "group workers," "community organizers," or "consultants in problems of ——." They are no longer social workers, not even in name.

It would be regrettable if such a scenario occurred. Social work, in private as well as agency practice, has something unique to offer, a value orientation. More than any other profession, social work considers the whole person in society rather than a segment of it. However, pocketbook issues could make the scenario a possibility for many practitioners, regardless of their ideals. Workers would not be happy with their profession if they have invested a considerable portion of their life's savings in establishing a private office, have forsaken secure agency jobs, and have been devoted to improving their education to provide marketable services to people who want to pay for them, only to see all these efforts come to nothing because they belong to a profession that is not recognized as being of value.

With increased competition from professional groups and decreased third-party support, practitioners must rely more than ever on their professional group. Though many practitioners seem to think otherwise, the profession and its organizations are necessary to the viability of private practice. Without a social work affiliation, private practitioners would have no more influence and credibility than do the many self-proclaimed "psychotherapists" and unregulated counselors that now abound. Without a professional affiliation, the private practitioner would have a hard time claiming an expertise or convincing potential clients of high ethical and professional standards. Professional affiliation is the only realistic way to compete effectively against other professional groups.

Unfortunately, many private practitioners do not seem convinced that their careers are intertwined with that of the profession. They devote their efforts to convincing potential clients that they have a worthwhile service to offer and have little concern for the well-being of the profession as a whole. A high proportion are not NASW members, and many do not belong to any other social work organization. Some private practitioners who retain NASW membership contribute little more than their annual dues. In the long run, this is self-defeating. Their lack of support causes the profession to lose influence, which, in turn, reduces the "drawing power" of the individual private practitioner as well as reduces the chances of third-party reimbursement.

Even with the support of every private practitioner, the profession will have a difficult time achieving its goals. It is working toward them from a weaker position than in times past. The public and private social agencies have endured enormous funding cutbacks that have led to considerable personnel reductions. In 1973, Gruber predicted that 25 percent of the voluntary agencies, in only five years, would no longer exist.[15] Many of those surviving are holding on by utilizing more volunteers and less well-trained personnel. Many agencies now rely on funds from insurance company payments for direct client services rather than from their traditional sources of revenue—voluntary contributions and government grants. This means they are more likely to hire only those individuals and professionals who have eligible insurance credentials. With fewer social work jobs at the entry level and fewer opportunities for advancement once a social work job is obtained, there is less incentive for people to enter the profession. This means a smaller membership base for the profession and a commensurate decline in its influence.[16]

Goals for the Future of Private Practice

No matter how weak or strong a professional association is, it would have little appeal to private consumers and third parties unless it could show that its members adhered to high standards. Usually, this is shown by public regulations such as licensing, peer preview, competency tests, and measurably effective methods. Social workers in private practice would have little incentive for remaining in the profession if the standards were lacking. Therefore, private practitioners, working through the professional association, have a great stake in further upgrading professional standards, improving quality controls, and developing the way their practice is publicly regulated. As these goals are achieved, there is greater likelihood that consumers will continue to seek their services and third parties will be more inclined to help finance it. There is an optimistic future for social work and its private practice sector once it reaches its elusive goals of improved standards and quality controls and can effectively demonstrate this to consumers and insurers.

To achieve a productive and vital private practice, the profession and its members must further improve quality standards. Great efforts have been made, and many successes have already been achieved by the profession in the past few years toward this end, but there is still much to be done. Consumers and those who pay for professional services will question any practitioner who cannot demonstrate that such standards exist. Private practitioners, regardless of their individual qualities, are having a difficult time showing potential consumers and third parties that their profession, compared to other professions, is worthy of patronage. From the private practitioner's viewpoint, five major quality assurance objectives must still be accomplished. Implicit in each goal is the belief that their achievement will benefit the profession as well as private practitioners.

Objective 1: Competency Exams for All NASW Members

The first goal is to test all applicants for membership in NASW. This proposed exam is not the same as the ACSW test and is not suggested as a replacement for it. Most NASW members have taken no NASW-sponsored tests to demonstrate professional competency.

Currently, only about half the NASW members are also in ACSW.[17] Social workers who became ACSW-certified before 1971 are not required to take the exam to retain their membership. Baccalaureate-level social workers, MSWs without the required experience, and experienced social workers without other qualifications also do not take the ACSW exam. This means to the consumer and to third parties that affiliation with the professional association does not, in itself, provide much quality assurance. If a professional association is to have much credibility, it must tell the public that it distinguishes between those who are qualified for membership and those who are not. Most professions use competency tests as well as education and experience to qualify for membership. This permits them to make the claim, whether or not it is valid, that all their members have proved a certain degree of competence. NASW is one of the few professional associations that cannot make such a claim. Someone can become an NASW member almost automatically through status as a student in an accredited school of social work or by graduating from the school. Others can become members without graduate education by working in the right agency setting. In effect, this implies to the public that social agencies and the schools of social work rather than the professional organization itself determines who its members will be. A profession that, in reality, does not screen its membership will obviously have more difficulty convincing consumers, regulators, and third parties that the profession is rigorous in its quality controls.

NASW has not developed competency tests as a requirement for membership largely because of the disparate nature of its membership. There are so many different kinds of social workers, with various levels of training, experience, and areas of expertise, that one test for all of them seems unfair and inapplicable. The profession has also found it difficult to develop an exam that tests competence for each of these various sectors and that distinguishes between those who should and should not belong. This argument should be vitiated now that the ACSW exam has tested for competency for many years, and since several states have had competency exams for social workers. If it can be done by them, it can be done by the professional association. To encompass all the groups who are NASW members, the exam could consist of two discrete parts. One part could test general social work knowledge, its history and philosophy, values and generic principles. This should be given to all applicants, regardless of their educational levels, work experience, or fields of practice. Those who pass this exam and meet the other qualifications would be eligible for NASW membership. A second exam could be taken by only those NASW members who want to demonstrate competence in a specialty. Like many other professional organizations, NASW could have various specialty boards whose members would design the exams. These tests could focus on the area of expertise needed for practice. The association would, as a result, be able to claim all its members have demonstrated a general competence and that many of its members have demonstrated a competence in some specialty as well.

Objective 2: Periodic Reexaminations

The second goal is to demonstrate to the public that the professional social worker has been keeping up with advances in knowledge. All dynamic professions have an expanding knowledge base, and improved technology and the credibility of the profession is largely contingent upon the ability to show that its members are current. If there is no way to demonstrate that a member is still competent, it implies to the consumer that the profession is stagnant in its growth of knowledge. This is not an effective way to attract clients or to retain the approbation of third parties. Periodic reexaminations are the customary way to prove that one has retained competence and are required of most other professionals and occupational groups. Even people who want to keep driving their cars must demonstrate continued competence. But there is no such requirement for social workers. Other professions, through their professional associations as well as through state licensing, require proof of continued competence and use exams every five to ten years after the first competency tests have been passed. There is no reason why the same tests for initial entry into the profession or the specialty could not also be given to experienced social workers at least once every decade. Obviously passing the exam does not in itself prove that the person is competent to do social work or that those who fail it or do not take it are no longer competent, but it has some value in providing some assurances for the consumer.

Objective 3: Continuing Education Requirements

Another facet of demonstrating that the practitioner has kept current is through continuing education. It has been pointed out that continuing education does not prove continuing competence, but taking courses and studying certainly suggest to consumers that the practitioner wants to keep current.[18] But what is the vehicle for showing the consumer that such motivation exists? The consumer is entitled to the assurance that professional membership itself is evidence that the practitioner has kept current. Recognizing this, most of the other professions enforce the requirement that their members take a specified number of continuing education courses periodically. NASW does too, but as discussed in chapter 4, it uses the "honor system" for its enforcement. Some professions keep computerized records of the number of formal credits each member has acquired; when a member applies for renewal, their CEU credits are scrutinized and, if they have not obtained sufficient credits, they are put on probation until they have fulfilled the requirement. This record keeping is not expensive for a professional association, and its costs are met by the member. NASW's system does not always assure consumers and third parties that the social work member has kept current.

Objective 4: Eliminate 'Grandfathering'

In chapter 4, it was pointed out that social workers who were certified before 1971 are excused from the obligation to take the ACSW exam. Furthermore, in most states that have competency exams for workers who apply to be licensed, the veteran practitioners are not required to take the test to get the license. In both cases, they retain their membership through "grandfathering," with no other demonstration that they are competent or have kept up to date. The rationale that veteran social workers have proved their knowledge through experience is very unconvincing. If social workers actually believe this, it certainly does not mean that consumer groups do—it is hard to believe that many social workers do either. One suspects that a latent reason for grandfathering is to protect more experienced social workers from the embarrassment of failing the exams. Experienced social workers may want grandfathering because they doubt that fair exams can be devised. This may be a valid concern, but then it should be valid and equally applicable to newer social workers as well. The profession's leadership is still dominated by social workers who have been grandfathered, so they may not want to change this requirement, but, as long as it continues to exist in professional certification as well in state licensing, it makes it that much more difficult for social workers to claim rigor in their quality controls.

Objective 5: Expand and Upgrade Licensing

Finally, the elusive goal of meaningful public regulation for social work practice in every state must be reached. Consumers and third parties will certainly not continue to support any professional group whose practice is not regulated through licensing.[19] NASW members have been active in every state to get licensing and to improve existing licensing. Yet, almost half the states are still not licensed, and few of the others are based on laws that actually distinguish competent practice from that which is not. From the private practitioner's view, achieving this goal is crucial; perhaps the private practitioner has more at stake in improving the licensing situation than any other social worker and is thus more obligated to work harder toward its realization.

There are, of course, many other goals that private social work practitioners have sought to improve their position. Many have advocated that private practice be restricted to those with advanced social work degrees or special additional training. This would counter the argument raised by some competing professionals that social workers should not be patronized or reimbursed by third parties because they lack the high level of training that is required of other professional groups. Many practitioners have advocated that the profession develop fairly autonomous subspecialties for practitioners who want to provide particular clinical services. They argue that they have no way at present to demonstrate that they are competent to provide valuable services. Many private practitioners advocate a closer, mutually supportive relationship with agency-based colleagues than now exists. They argue that the well-being of private practitioners and that of all other social workers will be improved with more mutual support and respect. These goals, however, are controversial, and efforts to achieve them will distract from the far more immediate ones listed above. The five objectives have to be given priority because failure to achieve them in the near future could seriously impair the prospects for social work and its private practice.

Conclusion

Exciting and challenging days lie ahead for social work and its private practitioners. The excitement will come from effectively competing with other professions so that social work can continue to provide its valuable services in private as well as agency practice. The challenge will be in finding ways of upgrading quality assurances so the competition can occur. It is, of course, always easier to say what ought to be done than to do it. But it seems likely that quality assurance efforts—licensing, competency exams, reexaminations, peer review, and continuing education requirements—will receive more serious attention by all social workers as the competition continues to intensify. If social workers redouble their efforts to demonstrate the value and quality of its services, the prospects for the profession are encouraging. If it takes this course, then social work can continue to provide worthy and effective assistance for the problems that plague mankind.

Notes and References

1. Arnold M. Levin, "Private Practice Is Alive and Well," *Social Work*, 21 (September 1976), p. 361.

2. Robert Barker, "Supply Side Economics in Private Psychotherapy Practice: Some Ominous and Encouraging Trends," *Psychotherapy in Private Practice*, 1 (Spring 1983), pp. 71–81.

3. Martin Gross, *The Psychological Society* (New York: Random House, 1978), pp. 50–51.

4. U.S. Congress, Office of Technology Assessment, *Background Paper No. 3: The Efficacy and Effectiveness of Psychotherapy. Cost Effectiveness Analysis of Medical Technology* (Washington, D.C.: U.S. Government Printing Office, 1980), pp. 4–6.

5. U.S. Department of Health and Human Services, *Health Resources Studies: Report on Health Personnel in the United States* (Washington, D.C.: U.S. Government Printing Office, 1982), pp. 77–98.

6. Ibid., pp. 151–152.

7. W. Lazarus et al., "Competition Among Health Practitioners: The Influence of the Medical Profession on the Health Manpower Market," *Report of the Federal Trade Commission* (Washington, D.C.: U.S. Government Printing Office, 1981), pp. ii–9.

8. Louise Enoch and George Sigel, "Third-Party Reimbursements: Countertherapeutic Considerations," *Psychiatric Opinion,* 16 (July 1979), pp. 8–16.

9. National Association of Social Workers, "Inouye Seeks Proclamation," *NASW News,* 28 (July 1983), p. 4.

10. Janet Asher, "The Coming Exclusion of Counselors from the Mental Health Care System," *CEU Clearinghouse* (College Park, Md.: Maryland Foundation, Summer 1980), pp. 3–19.

11. Charles Goodstein, "Insurance Reimbursement," *Psychiatric News,* 18 (June 17, 1983), p. 2.

12. Jack Rothman, "Macro Social Work in a Tightening Economy," *Social Work,* 24 (July 1979), pp. 274–281.

13. Robert Cassidy, "Will the PPO Movement Freeze You Out?" *Medical Economics,* April 18, 1983, pp. 86–89.

14. Mark Holoweiko, "A Doomsday Timetable for Independent Practice," *Medical Economics,* June 27, 1983, pp. 31–40.

15. Alan R. Gruber, "The High Cost of Delivering Services," *Social Work,* 18 (July 1973), pp. 33–40.

16. Catherine Born, "Coping with an Environment of Scarcity: Graduate Social Work Programs and Responses to Current Crises," *Journal of Education for Social Work,* 18 (Fall 1982), pp. 5–13.

17. Ruth R. Middleman, *A Study Guide for ACSW Certification* (Washington, D.C.: National Association of Social Workers, 1981), p. 8.

18. Richard L. Edwards and Ronald K. Green, "Mandatory Continuing Education: Time for Reevaluation," *Social Work,* 28 (January–February 1983), pp. 43–48.

19. David A. Hardcastle, "Public Regulation of Social Work," *Social Work,* 22 (January 1977), pp. 14–20. See also National Association of Social Workers, "States with Acts Regulating Social Work," *NASW News,* 29 (May 1984), p. 3.

bibliography

Accounting and Financial Reporting. Alexandria, Va.: United Way of America, 1979.

Alexander, Chauncey. "Testimony to Subcommittee on Comprehensive Coverage." New York: Health Insurance Association of America, 1976.

Allison, James, and Hartman, Klaus. "A Note on Choosing a Service Provider from Telephone Listings," *Journal of Counseling Psychology,* 9 (January 1981), pp. 78–80.

American Association of Social Workers. Memorandum, May 3, 1926. Unpublished document.

Aptekar, Herbert. "Supervision and the Development of Professional Responsibility: An Application of Systems Thought," *Jewish Social Work Forum,* 3 (Fall 1965), pp. 4–17.

Asher, Janet. "The Coming Exclusion of Counselors from the Mental Health Care System," *CEU Clearinghouse.* College Park, Md.: The Maryland Foundation, Summer 1980.

Ayers, George W.; Mindel, Charles H.; Robinson, Linda; and Wright, Johnny. "Fees in a Human Service Agency: Why Do Clients Pay?" *Social Work,* 26 (May 1981), pp. 245–248.

Barkan, Theresa W. "Private Casework Practice in a Medical Clinic," *Social Work,* 18 (July 1973), pp. 5–9.

Barker, Robert L. *The Business of Psychotherapy: Private Practice Administration for Therapists, Counselors, and Social Workers.* New York: Columbia University Press, 1982.

——. "Research Findings Related to the Education of Baccalaureate Social Workers," in Robert L. Barker and Thomas Briggs, eds., *Undergraduate Social Work Education for Practice.* Vol. 2. Washington, D.C.: U.S. Government Printing Office and U.S. Veterans Administration, 1971.

——. "Supply Side Economics in Private Psychotherapy Practice: Some Ominous and Encouraging Trends," *Psychotherapy in Private Practice,* 1 (Spring 1983), pp. 71–81.

———. "The Tarasoff Paradox: Confidentiality and the Duty to Warn," *Social Thought,* 10 (to be published 1984).

———. *Treating Couples in Crisis: Fundamentals and Practice in Marital Therapy.* New York: Free Press, 1984.

Barker, Robert, and Briggs, Thomas. *Differential Use of Social Work Manpower: An Analysis and Manpower Study.* New York: National Association of Social Workers, 1968.

———. *Using Teams to Deliver Social Services.* Syracuse, N.Y.: Syracuse University Press, 1969.

Barker, Robert; Briggs, Thomas; and Daly, Dorothy Bird. *Educating the Undergraduate for Professional Social Work Roles.* Syracuse, N.Y.: Syracuse University Press, 1969.

Bartlett, Harriett M. "Toward Clarification and Improvement of Social Work Practice," *Social Work,* 3 (April 1958), pp. 3–9.

Baumback, Clifford, and Lawyer, Kenneth. *How to Organize and Operate a Small Business.* 7th ed. Englewood Cliffs, N.J.: Prentice-Hall, 1983.

Bentrup, Walter C. "The Profession and the Means Test," *Social Work,* 9 (April 1964), pp. 10–17.

Berkowitz, Sidney. "Reaction of Clients and Caseworkers toward Fees," *Journal of Social Casework,* 27 (March 1947), p. 144.

Bernstein, Barton E. "Malpractice: An Ogre on the Horizon," *Social Work,* 23 (March 1978), pp. 106–112.

———. "Privileged Communications to the Social Worker," *Social Work,* 22 (July 1977), pp. 264–268.

Borenzweig, Herman. "Agency vs. Private Practice: Similarities and Differences," *Social Work,* 26 (May 1981), pp. 239–244.

———. "Who Passes the California Licensing Examinations?" *Social Work,* 22 (May 1977), pp. 173–177.

Born, Catherine. "Coping with an Environment of Scarcity: Graduate Social Work Programs and Responses to Current Crises," *Journal of Education for Social Work,* 18 (Fall 1982), pp. 5–13.

Bowen, Murray. *Family Therapy in Clinical Practice.* New York: Jason Aronson, 1978.

Brager, George, and Barr, Sherman. "Perceptions and Reality—The Poor Man's View of Social Services," in Brager and F. P. Purcell, eds., *Community Action Against Poverty.* New Haven, Conn.: College & University Press, 1967.

Bramhall, Martha, and Ezell, Susan. "How Burned Out Are You?" *Public Welfare,* 39 (Winter 1981), pp. 23–27.

Briar, Scott. "The Age of Accountability," *Social Work,* 18 (January 1973), pp. 2 and 114.

———. "Family Services," in Henry S. Maas, ed., *Five Fields of Social Service: Review of Research.* New York: National Association of Social Workers, 1966.

Briggs, Thomas L. "A Critique of the NASW Manpower Statement," *Journal of Education for Social Work,* 10 (Winter 1975), pp. 5–19.

———. "Private Practice," Memorandum to Chapter Chairmen, Document No. 3832/1/5. New York: National Association of Social Workers, 1961.

Brigham, Eugene. *Financial Management.* 2d ed. Hinsdale, Ill.: Dryden Press, 1979.

Browning, C. H. *Private Practice Handbook: The Tools and Techniques for Successful Practice Development.* 2d ed. Los Alamitos, Calif.: Duncliffs, 1982.

Burns, Eveline. "Some Economic Aspects of Welfare as an Institution," in John Romanyshyn, ed., *Social Science and Social Welfare.* New York: Council on Social Work Education, 1974.

Buttrick, Shirley. "Innovative Ideas in Social Service Delivery," *The Social Welfare Forum, 1972.* New York: National Conference on Social Welfare and Columbia University Press, 1972.

Carbino, Rosemarie, and Morgenbesser, Mel. "A National Challenge: The Decline in MSW Admission Applications," *Journal of Education for Social Work,* 18 (Fall 1982), pp. 14–22.

Cassidy, Robert. "Will the PPO Movement Freeze You Out?" *Medical Economics,* 60 (April 18, 1983), pp. 86–89.

Cloward, Richard, and Epstein, Irwin. "Social Welfare's Disengagement from the Poor," in Mayer Zald, ed., *Social Welfare Institutions.* New York: John Wiley & Sons, 1965.

Cloward, Richard, and Piven, Frances Fox. "Notes toward a Radical Social Work," in Roy Bailey and Mike Brake, eds., *Radical Social Work.* New York: Pantheon Books, 1975.

Cohen, Michael. "The Emergence of Private Practice in Social Work," *Social Problems,* 14 (Summer 1966), pp. 84–93.

———. "Some Characteristics of Social Workers in Private Practice," *Social Work,* 11 (April 1966), pp. 69–77.

Cohen, Nathan E. "A Changing Profession in a Changing World," *Social Work,* 1 (October 1956), p. 12–19.

Condie, C. David; Hanson, Janet A.; Lang, Nanci E.; Moss, Deanna K.; and Kane, Rosalie A. "How the Public Views Social Work," *Social Work,* 23 (January 1978), pp. 47–53.

Constable, Robert. "New Directions in Social Work Education," *Journal of Education for Social Work,* 14 (Winter 1978), pp. 23–32.

Cookerly, J. R., and McClaren, K. *How to Increase Your Private Practice Power.* Ft. Worth, Tex.: Center for Counseling and Developmental Services, 1982.

Coulton, Claudia. "Quality Assurance for Social Service Programs: Lessons from Health Care," *Social Work,* 27 (September 1982), pp. 397–402.

———. *Social Work Quality Assurance Programs: A Comparative Analysis.* Washington, D.C.: National Association of Social Workers, 1979.

Diagnostic and Statistical Manual of Mental Disorders (3d ed.; Washington, D.C.: American Psychiatric Association, 1980).

Dinerman, Miriam. *Social Work Curriculum at the Baccalaureate and Master's Levels.* New York: Lois & Samuel Silberman Fund, 1981.

Drucker, Ruth, and King, Diana. "Private Practice Services for Low-Income People," *Social Work,* 18 (March 1973), pp. 115–118.

Dubin, S. S. "Obsolescence or Lifelong Education: A Choice for the Professional," *American Psychologist,* 36 (June 1981), p. 486.

Edwards, Richard L., and Green, Ronald K. "Mandatory Continuing Education: Time for Reevaluation," *Social Work,* 28 (January–February 1983), pp. 43–48.

Enoch, Louise, and Sigel, George. "Third-Party Reimbursements: Countertherapeutic Considerations," *Psychiatric Opinion,* 16 (July 1979), pp. 8–16.

Epstein, Laura. "Is Autonomous Practice Possible?" *Social Work,* 18 (March 1973), pp. 5–12.

Everett, Craig. "The Master's Degree in Marriage and Family Therapy," *Journal of Marital and Family Therapy,* 5 (July 1979), pp. 7–14.

Ewalt, Patricia L. "Policy Issues in Financing Mental Health Services," *Social Work,* 24 (July 1979), pp. 283–290.

Fandetti, Donald V. "Income versus Service Strategies," *Social Work,* 17 (January 1972), pp. 87–93.

Fanning, John P. "Protection of Privacy and Fair Information Practices," *The Social Welfare Forum, 1975.* New York: National Conference on Social Welfare and Columbia University Press, 1976.

Farber, Barry, and Heifetz, Louis. "The Satisfaction and Stresses of Psychotherapeutic Work: A Factor Analytic Study," *Professional Psychology,* 12 (October 1981), pp. 621–628.

Feldstein, Donald. "Debate on Private Practice," *Social Work,* 22 (January 1977), p. 3.

——. "Do We Need Professions in Our Society? Professionalization versus Consumerism," *Social Work,* 16 (October 1971), pp. 5–11.

Fischer, Joel, ed. *The Effectiveness of Social Casework.* Springfield, Ill.: Charles C Thomas, Publisher, 1976.

Fizdale, Ruth. "Formalizing the Relationship between Private Practitioners and Social Agencies," *Social Casework,* 40 (November 1959), pp. 539–544.

———. "The Rising Demand for Private Casework Services," *Social Welfare Forum, 1961.* New York: National Conference on Social Welfare and Columbia University Press, 1961.

Foley, Henry, and Sharfstein, Steven. *Madness and Government: Who Cares for the Mentally Ill?* Washington, D.C.: American Psychiatric Press, 1983.

Foreman, Bruce, and Foreman, Kadett. "Market Concepts for Psychotherapists," *Psychotherapy in Private Practice,* 1 (Fall 1983).

"45 Landmark Decisions," *Family Therapy News,* 14 (May 1983), p. 8. (Reprinted from *Family Advocate,* 5 [Summer 1982], pp. 4–5.)

Freudenberger, Herbert. "Hazards of Psychotherapeutic Practice," *Psychotherapy in Private Practice,* 1 (Spring 1983), pp. 83–91.

Freudenberger, Herbert, and Richelson, Geraldine. *Burnout: The High Cost of Achievement.* New York: Doubleday, Anchor Press, 1980.

Getzel, George S. "Speculations on the Crisis in Social Work Recruitment: Some Modest Proposals," *Social Work,* 28 (May–June 1983), pp. 235–237.

Goldberg, Arthur, and Kovac, David. "A New Concept of Subsidy in Determining Fees for Service," *Social Casework,* 52 (April 1971), pp. 206–219.

Goldberg, Martin. "To Incorporate or Not to Incorporate: Now It's a Question," *Medical Economics,* December 7, 1981, p. 242.

Golton, Margaret A. "Private Practice in Social Work," *Encyclopedia of Social Work.* Vol. 2. 16th issue. New York: National Association of Social Workers, 1971.

Goodman, Nathaniel. "Are There Differences Between Fee and Non-Fee Cases?" *Social Work,* 4 (October 1960), pp. 46–52.

——. "Fee Charging," *Encyclopedia of Social Work.* Vol. 1. 16th issue. New York: National Association of Social Workers, 1971.

Goodstein, Charles. "Insurance Reimbursement," *Psychiatric News,* June 17, 1983, p. 6.

Gorlick, Sheldon. "Tax Audits: How to Dodge the IRS Bullet," *Medical Economics,* January 24, 1983, pp. 171–174.

Grace, William. *The ABCs of IRAs.* New York: Dell Publishing Co., 1982.

Green, Ronald K., and Cox, Gibbi. "Social Work and Malpractice: A Converging Course," *Social Work,* 23 (March 1978), pp. 100–105.

Gross, Martin. *The Psychological Society.* New York: Random House, 1978.

Gruber, Alan R. "The High Cost of Delivering Services," *Social Work,* 18 (July 1973), pp. 33–40.

Hardcastle, David A. "Public Regulation of Social Work," *Social Work,* 22 (January 1977), pp. 14–20.

Hardman, Dale G. "Mr. Pringle's Shingle," *Social Work,* 23 (January 1978), pp. 3–4.

Henderson, Reed, and Shore, Barbara K. "Accountability for What and to Whom?" *Social Work,* 19 (July 1974), pp. 387–388, 507.

Hendrickson, D. E.; Janney, S. P.; and Fraze, J. E. *How to Establish Your Own Private Practice.* Muncie, Ind.: Contemporary Press, 1978.

Hofstadter, Richard. *Social Darwinism in American Thought.* Philadelphia: University of Pennsylvania Press, 1944.

Hofstein, Saul. "Changing Social Structure," *Social Work,* 7 (April 1962), pp. 94–95.

Holoweiko, Mark. "A Doomsday Timetable for Independent Practice," *Medical Economics,* June 23, 1983, pp. 31–40.

Houle, Cyril. *Continuing Learning in the Professions.* San Francisco: Jossey-Bass, 1980.

Howe, Elizabeth. "Public Professions and the Private Model of Professionalism," *Social Work,* 25 (May 1980), pp. 179–191.

Internal Revenue Service. *Tax Guide for Small Businesses.* Washington, D.C.: U.S. Government Printing Office, 1984.

Johnson, Donald. "Legal Regulation of the Social Work Profession," *Social Casework,* 51 (November 1970), pp. 551–555.

Johnson, Frank M., Jr. "Court Decisions and the Social Services," *Social Work,* 20 (September 1975), pp. 343–347.

Keefe, Thomas. "The Economic Context of Empathy," *Social Work,* 23 (November 1978), pp. 460–465.

Kilgore, James. "Establishing and Maintaining a Private Practice," *Journal of Marriage and Family Counseling,* 1 (April 1975), pp. 145–148.

Koret, Sydney. "The Social Worker in Private Practice," *Social Work,* 3 (July 1958), pp. 11–17.

Kurzman, Paul A. "Private Practice as a Social Work Function," *Social Work,* 21 (September 1976), pp. 363–368.

Lantz, James E., and Lenahan, Beverly. "Referral-Fatigue Therapy," *Social Work,* 21 (May 1976), pp. 239–240.

Lazarus, W., et al. *Competition Among Health Practitioners: The Influence of the Medical Profession on the Health Manpower Market,* Report of the Federal Trade Commission. Washington, D.C.: U.S. Government Printing Office, 1981.

Lee, Judith. "Weeping for the Lost Profession: Social Work in Transition," *Jewish Social Work Forum,* 19 (Spring 1983), pp. 20–32.

Levenstein, Sidney. *Private Practice in Social Casework: A Profession's Changing Pattern.* New York: Columbia University Press, 1964.

Levin, Arnold M. "Private Practice Is Alive and Well," *Social Work,* 21 (September 1976), pp. 356–362.

——. *Psychotherapy Private Practice.* New York: Free Press, 1983.

Levitan, Stephan, and Kornfield, Donald. "Clinical and Cost Benefits of Liaison Psychiatry," *American Journal of Psychiatry,* 138 (June 1981), pp. 790–793.

Levy, Charles S. "The Ethics of Supervision," *Social Work,* 18 (March 1973), pp. 14–21.

Lewin, Mark H. *Establishing and Maintaining a Successful Professional Practice.* Rochester, N.Y.: Professional Development Institute, 1978.

———. "Learning to Market Services," *Professional Psychology,* 7 (May 1976), pp. 243–245.

Lindenberg, Ruth Ellen. "Hard to Reach: Client or Casework Agency?" *Social Work,* 3 (October 1958), pp. 23–29.

Lorish, Claudia C. "Examining Quality Assurance Systems," *Health and Social Work,* 2 (May 1977), pp. 20–41.

Lubove, Roy. *The Professional Altruist: The Emergence of Social Work as a Career: 1890–1930.* Cambridge, Mass.: Harvard University Press, 1965.

Marcus, Lotte. "Communication Concepts and Principles," in John Turner, ed., *Social Work Treatment: Interlocking Theoretical Approaches.* New York: Free Press, 1979.

McCann, Charles W., and Cutler, Jane Park. "Ethics and the Alleged Unethical," *Social Work,* 24 (January 1979), pp. 5–8.

Meenaghan, Thomas M., and Mascari, Michael. "Consumer Choice, Consumer Control in Service Delivery," *Social Work,* 16 (October 1971), pp. 50–57.

Meltzer, M. L. "Insurance Reimbursement: A Mixed Blessing," *American Psychologist,* 30 (1975), pp. 1151–1164.

Merle, Sherman. "Some Arguments Against Private Practice," *Social Work,* 7 (January 1962), pp. 12–17.

Meyer, Carol H. "What Directions for Direct Practice?" *Social Work,* 24 (July 1979), pp. 267–272.

Middleman, Ruth R. *A Study Guide for ACSW Certification.* Washington, D.C.: National Association of Social Workers, 1981.

Mone, Louis. *Private Practice: A Professional Business.* La Jolla, Calif.: Elm Press, 1983.

National Association of Social Workers. "Association Assists Members in Litigation On Right To Practice," *NASW News,* 26 (November 1981), p. 10.

——. "CHAMPUS Experiment: Survey Supports Vendorship," *NASW News,* 27 (October 1982), p. 8.

——. "Council Proposes Definition, Standards for Clinicians," *NASW News,* 28 (May 1983), p. 13.

——. "The Definition of Clinical Social Work," *NASW News,* 28 (May 1983), p. 13.

——. *Handbook on the Private Practice of Social Work.* Washington, D.C.: National Association of Social Workers, 1974.

——. "Inouye Seeks Proclamation," *NASW News,* 28 (July 1983), p. 4.

——. "Legislative Moves Toward Licensure Continue Unabated," *NASW News,* 20 (September 1975), p. 12.

——. "Manpower Data Bank Frequency Distributions." Washington, D.C.: National Association of Social Workers, 1975.

——. *Manual for the Adjudication of Grievances.* Rev. ed. Washington, D.C.: National Association of Social Workers, 1973.

——. "NASW Adopts Continuing Education Standards," *NASW News,* 27 (September 1982), pp. 20–21.

——. "The NASW Code of Ethics," *Social Work,* 25 (May 1980), pp. 184–188.

——. *NASW Register of Clinical Social Workers.* 3d ed. Silver Spring, Md.: National Association of Social Workers, 1982.

——. "New Policy Statement on Licensing Issued," *NASW News,* 19 (September 1974), p. 12.

——. *Procedures for the Adjudication of Grievances.* Washington, D.C.: National Association of Social Workers, 1970, rev. 1978.

——. "Regulatory Bills See Light of Day," *NASW News,* 28 (May 1983), p. 1.

——. "Standards for Continuing Professional Education," *NASW Policy Statement No. 10.* Silver Spring, Md.: National Association of Social Workers, 1982.

——. "Standards for the Regulation of Social Work Practice," *NASW Policy Statement No. 5.* Washington, D.C.: National Association of Social Workers, 1975.

——. "Working Statement on the Purpose of Social Work," *Social Work,* 26 (January 1981), p. 6.

Nichols, William. "Doctoral Programs in Marital and Family Therapy," *Journal of Marital and Family Therapy,* 5 (July 1979), pp. 23–28.

Niswonger, C. Rollin, and Fess, Philip. *Accounting Principles.* 12th ed. Cincinnati, Ohio: Southwestern Publishing Co., 1979.

Noll, John. "Needed—A Bill of Rights for Clients," *Professional Psychologist,* 5 (May 1974), pp. 3–12.

——. "The Psychotherapist and Informed Consent," *American Journal of Psychiatry,* 133 (December 1976), pp. 1451–1453.

Oppenheimer, Irene. "Third-Party Payments," *Social Policy,* 8 (November–December 1977), pp. 55–58.

Page, Alfred N. "Economics and Social Work: A Neglected Relationship," *Social Work,* 22 (January 1977), pp. 48–53.

Palmer, Ted B. "Matching Worker and Client in Corrections," *Social Work,* 18 (March 1973), pp. 95–103.

Peek, Josephine, and Plotkin, Charlotte. "Social Caseworkers in Private Practice," *Smith College Studies in Social Work,* 21 (March 1951), pp. 165–197.

Perlman, Helen, et al. "Psychotherapy and Counseling," *Annals of the New York Academy of Sciences,* 63 (1955), pp. 319–432.

Piliavin, Irving. "Restructuring the Provision of Social Services," *Social Work,* 13 (January 1968), pp. 34–41.

Pines, Ayala, and Kafry, Ditsa. "Occupational Tedium in the Social Services," *Social Work,* 23 (November 1978), pp. 499–507.

Pins, Arnulf M. "Changes in Social Work Education and Their Implications for Practice," *Social Work,* 16 (April 1971).

Piven, Frances Fox, and Cloward, Richard. *Regulating the Poor: The Functions of Social Welfare.* New York: Random House, 1971.

Pruger, Robert. "The Good Bureaucrat," *Social Work,* 18 (July 1973), pp. 26–32.

Richan, Willard C., and Mendelsohn, Allan R. *Social Work: The Unloved Profession.* New York: Franklin Watts, 1973.

Richmond, Mary. *Friendly Visiting among the Poor.* New York: Macmillan Co., 1899.

———. *Social Diagnosis.* New York: Russell Sage Foundation, 1917.

———. *What Is Social Casework?* New York: Russell Sage Foundation, 1922.

———. "Why Case Records?" *The Family,* 6 (November 1925), pp. 214–216.

Robinowitz, Carolyn, and Greenblatt, Milton. "Continuing Certification and Continuing Education," *American Journal of Psychiatry,* 137 (March 1980), pp. 292–301.

Rockmore, Myron. "Private Practice: An Exploratory Inquiry," *Survey,* 84 (1948), pp. 109–111.

Rosenfeld, Jona M. "The Domain and Expertise of Social Work: A Conceptualization," *Social Work,* 28 (May–June 1983), pp. 186–191.

Roth, Herbert. "Independent Practice," *Family Therapy News,* 14 (May 1983), p. 8.

Roth, Loren, and Meisel, Alan. "Dangerousness, Confidentiality, and the Duty to Warn," *American Journal of Psychiatry,* 134 (May 1977), pp. 508–511.

Rothman, Jack. "Macro Social Work in a Tightening Economy," *Social Work,* 24 (July 1979), pp. 274–281.

Ryerson, Rowena, and Weller, Elizabeth. "The Private Practice of Psychiatric Social Work," *Journal of Psychiatric Social Work,* 16 (1947), pp. 110–116.

Samuels, Richard. "I Bought His Private Practice," *Psychotherapy in Private Practice,* 1 (Spring 1983), pp. 105–108.

Schwartz, Edward E. "A Way To End the Means Test," *Social Work,* 9 (July 1964), pp. 3–12.

Schwartz, Harry. "Two Decades that Altered the Character of Medical Practice in America," *Medical Tribune,* 21 (May 7, 1980), p. 1.

Schwartz, William. "Private Troubles and Public Issues: One Social Work Job or Two?" *The Social Welfare Forum, 1969.* New York: National Conference on Social Welfare and Columbia University Press, 1969.

Scurfield, Raymond Monsour. "Clinician to Administrator: Difficult Role Transition?" *Social Work,* 26 (November 1981), pp. 495–501.

Seabury, Brett A. "Arrangement of Physical Space in Social Work Settings," *Social Work,* 16 (October 1971), pp. 43–49.

Selvini-Palazzoli, Mara, et al. "The Problem of the Referring Person," *Journal of Marriage and Family Therapy,* 6 (January 1980), pp. 3–10.

Shafer, Carl. "The Family Agency and the Private Casework Practitioner," *Social Casework,* 40 (November 1959), pp. 531–560.

Sharfstein, Steven. "Private Psychiatry and Accountability," *American Journal of Psychiatry,* 135 (November 1978), pp. 43–47.

Sharfstein, Steven; Taube, Carl; and Goldberg, Irving. "Problems in Analyzing the Comparative Costs of Private versus Public Psychiatric Care," *American Journal of Psychiatry,* 134 (January 1977), pp. 29–32.

Shear, Beatrix. *The Malpractice Problem for Non-Physician Health Care Professionals as Reflected in Professional Liability Rates.* Publication No. 573–88. Washington, D.C.: U.S. Department of Health, Education & Welfare, 1973.

Shireman, Joan. "Client and Worker Opinions about Fee-Charging in a Child Welfare Agency," *Child Welfare,* 54 (May 1975), pp. 331–340.

Siporin, Max. "Private Practice of Social Work: Functional Roles and Social Control," *Social Work,* 6 (April 1961), pp. 52–60.

Skinner, John. "Standards for the Private Practice of Psychotherapy by Psychiatric Social Workers," *Journal of Psychiatric Social Work,* 22 (January 1953), pp. 67–68.

Slovenko, Ralph, *Psychiatry and Law.* Boston: Little, Brown & Co, 1973.

Smalley, Ruth. "Can We Reconcile Generic Education and Specialized Practice?" *Journal of Psychiatric Social Work,* 23 (January 1954), pp. 207–214.

"Social Workers Professional Liability Insurance." New York: American Professional Agency, 1978.

Steiner, Gilbert. *The State of Welfare.* Washington, D.C.: The Brookings Institution, 1971.

Steiner, Lee R. "Casework as a Private Venture," *The Family,* 19 (March 1938), pp. 188–196.

———. "Hanging Out a Shingle," *Newsletter of the American Association of Psychiatric Social Workers,* 6 (Winter 1936), pp. 1–8. (Now *Journal of Psychiatric Social Work.*)

Stone, Anthony. "The Private Practice of Social Casework," *Social Work Journal,* 35 (January 1954), pp. 61–65.

Sullivan, Richard J. "Trends in Automated Social Services," *Social Work,* 27 (July 1982), pp. 359–361.

Swack, Lois G. "Continuing Education and Changing Needs," *Social Work,* 20 (November 1975), pp. 474–480.

Taibbi, Robert. "Supervisors as Mentors," *Social Work,* 28 (May–June 1983), pp. 237–238.

Tamkin, Arthur. "Adaptability: A Paramount Asset for Private Practice," *Professional Psychology,* 7 (November 1976), pp. 661–663.

Tennov, Dorothy. *Psychotherapy: The Hazardous Cure.* New York: Doubleday, Anchor Press, 1978.

Toren, Nina. "Semi-Professionalism and Social Work: A Theoretical Perspective," in Amitai Etzioni, ed., *The Semi-Professions and Their Organizations.* New York: Free Press, 1969.

Toseland, Ronald W., and Hacker, Lynda. "Self-Help Groups and Professional Involvement," *Social Work,* 27 (July 1982), pp. 341–347.

Trent, Chester, and Muhl, William. "Professional Liability Insurance and the American Psychiatrist," *American Journal of Psychiatry,* 132 (December 1975), pp. 1312–1315.

Tryon, Georgiana. "How Full-Time Practitioners Market Their Services: A National Survey," *Psychotherapy in Private Practice,* 1 (Spring 1983), pp. 91–100.

Turner, Francis. *Psychosocial Therapy: A Social Work Perspective.* New York: Free Press, 1978.

U.S. Congress, Office of Technology Assessment. *Background Paper No. 3: The Efficacy and Effectiveness of Psychotherapy. Cost Effectiveness Analysis of Medical Technology.* Washington, D.C.: U.S. Government Printing Office, 1980.

U.S. Department of Health, Education, and Welfare. *Credentialing Health Manpower.* Washington, D.C.: U.S. Government Printing Office, 1977.

——. *PSRO Program Manual.* Washington, D.C.: U.S. Government Printing Office, 1978.

U.S. Department of Health and Human Services. *Health Resources Studies: Report on Health Personnel in the United States.* Washington, D.C.: U.S. Government Printing Office, 1982.

————. *Medical Malpractice: Report of the Secretary's Commission on Malpractice.* Washington, D.C.: U.S. Government Printing Office, 1981.

Wallace, Marquis Earl. "Private Practice: A Nationwide Study," *Social Work,* 27 (May 1982), pp. 262–267.

Warfel, David J.; Maloney, Dennis M.; and Blase, Karen. "Consumer Feedback in Human Service Programs," *Social Work,* 26 (March 1981), pp. 151–156.

Weiner, Myron. *Human Services Management: Analysis and Applications.* Homewood, Ill.: Dorsey Press, 1982.

Weitz, Robert. "I Sold My Private Practice," *Psychotherapy in Private Practice,* 1 (Spring 1983), pp. 101–105.

index